THE
BELSPRING ROAD

Robert G. Bruce

Printed in the United States of America
Edited, formatted, and designed by Kristen Corrects, Inc.
Cover art design by Laurie Bruce and CreateSpace

First edition published 2018

ISBN-13: 978-0-692852262
ISBN-10: 692852263

THE BELSPRING ROAD

ROBERT G. BRUCE

CONTENTS

MAP OF BELSPRING

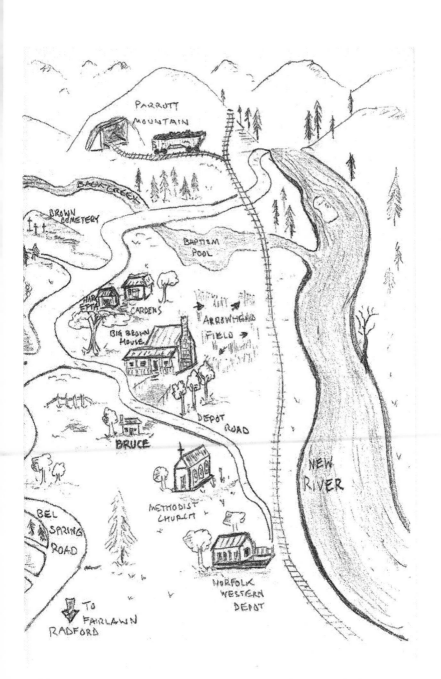

PREFACE

This collection of Appalachian mountain stories tells about the childhood of our family patriarch, Robert Wilson Bruce, of Belspring, Virginia, in the years from 1925 to 1940. To his children and grandchildren, he was Daddy and Paw-Paw, but for everyone else he was simply Bobby, an ordinary, good man; one of life's countless unknown people, never noted beyond a church membership roll or an obituary at death. But his life was rich and deep with the moral character, kindness, and love that make a man a gentleman and hero. This remembrance of him, with the events and people of which he told us, is our love letter to him.

This story, told through Bobby's voice, is not only a narrative about a young boy, it is also a stockpile of now largely forgotten accounts of a slice of life from the little southwestern Virginia communities of Belspring and its near neighbor, the coal mining town of Parrott, and of Bobby's days and years among the rascals and saints of those places. All those people, and Bobby too, are dead and gone, but a bit of their memory lives on in the tales that he told about them in their out-of-the-way part of the world.

By the 1990s, when Bobby was an old man, we often drove the back streets of those villages while he regaled me with details of the men and women and children who had once peopled those alleys and houses. When I remember this, I think of him as an amateur archeologist/anthropologist who unveils the layers of a life that is no more.

Today's world is shaped by TV, cell phones, and immediate communications that did not yet exist in the Belspring of the 1920s. Other than the occasional automobile, newspaper, or the N&W Railway down by the New River, life was insular, shaped by family and neighbors, church and schoolhouse. But once upon a time, Belspring and Parrott—like many other small places in bygone America—teemed with folks of all ages. They were lively villages boasting shops for car repair, house-fronts on which doctors hung their shingles, a schoolhouse and rail depot in walking distance of every child and adult, general stores that sold dry goods and groceries, a shoe repair shop run by two booze-hounds, a hot dog stand, and a barber shop on a back porch where hair was cut by the most famous cow-pasture baseball pitcher in those parts. Now, those villages and shops are mere shadows of that memorable past; only a few dozen houses remain, with scattered foundations on vacant lots, churches with aging congregations, and a few sad, unpainted storefronts. But blink your eyes and hovering over the whole village are the clouds of countless faded memories.

Though Bobby was a Christian man and looked forward to a heavenly home, that home to be—at least in his thoughts—did not have golden streets, but rather dirt and gravel lanes that looked like the alleys of the Belspring of yesteryear. In Bobby's mind, when the hymn said, *"There's a land that is fairer than day, and by faith we can see it afar,"*[1] it was a land that had the contours of the Belspring/Parrott he knew as a child.

Robert Gray Bruce,
eldest son of Robert (Bobby) Wilson Bruce

---

[1] "There's A Land that Is Fairer Than Day," Sanford Bennett, 1868

PART ONE

FAMILY

The abrupt end of childhood.

CHAPTER 1

My Mommie:
Nellie Vermilion Rowe Bruce

*The seminal event in my life, and the life of my family,
was Mommie's death. It was her life and death
that sheds light on the other stories and events that follow.
"Sometimes I feel like a motherless child."*

I CAME TO BELSPRING because Mommie killed herself. It was August of 1925 and my siblings and I were motherless children.

Even now in old age, this reality is hard to write, as if in the writing, it is once more engraved into my mind and heart. But it is a truth I need to tell my family and others who also deserve to hear.

My Mommie, Nellie Vermilion Rowe Bruce, the apple of her poppa William's eye, met George Cleveland Bruce when she was a mere child of thirteen.

"It was just like a fairy tale," she once told my older sister Margaret.

They met when Nellie and a friend were playing a game of house with their ragdolls down by the Norfolk & Western rail tracks near Nellie's house in Pearisburg,

Virginia. It was 1907, when along came a work car inspecting rail tracks.

George Cleveland Bruce, nineteen and handsome in a moon-faced way, was one of the inspectors. Eyes met; pleasantries were passed. Days became weeks and months during which Nellie and George left messages for one another under a big rock near the tracks. It was their secret life; four years later they eloped. Caught a train from Pearisburg's Liberty City station to Bristol, Tennessee and were married by the famous "marrying Methodist parson" A.H. Burroughs.

Nellie was a pretty, long-faced brunette. In her family of origin, she was the favored child and sister. For me and my siblings, she was Mommie, the moral center of our world and our family. She, Daddy, and the five of us children lived in the small Giles County, Virginia town of Pearisburg. At her death, I was eight years old, Margaret—twelve, Clyde—ten, Hazel—five, and Jimmy—two.

Our idyllic childhood ended on a tragic August morning in 1925; we were out in the neighborhood near the county fairgrounds, playing in the fields and ditches, in the woods or by the creeks not far from home. I thought all was right in my world of family, kin, friends, and our mountain town. For Mommie, it was obviously not that way.

At mid-morning on that day, for reasons we never knew, she drank Red Devil Lye, a substance used to unclog drains. The corrosive effect of the lye did not immediately kill her, and Doc Johnson later said she was for sure in terrible pain. In an attempt to complete her suicide, she went into our backyard and jumped down a dry, narrow, nineteen-foot well-water shaft, hoping the fall would end it. Neither did that work. A neighbor heard her moaning; the volunteer fire department was called and used a ladder to hoist her out of the shaft.

Immediately she was rushed to St. Elizabeth's Hospital in Pearisburg, only a half mile from our home. Doc did exploratory surgery and declared it hopeless; the fatal damage was done. He closed her up and started pain medication. I did not know these gruesome details for many years—really, until I was on the edge of being an old man and could allow myself to ponder her pain and death. After these eighty-five years without her or any explanation of why she preferred death, I can only suppose she tried to rid herself of some silent demon that plagued her. Sadly, one of the lasting effects of suicide is that the clarity of an answer never comes.

Mommie lingered for three or four days before the Grim Reaper claimed her. As she lay a'dying at St. Elizabeth's, the three eldest children—Margaret, Clyde, and I—were allowed to visit her. There she was in one of those old-fashioned, crank-up hospital beds; three other patients were in their beds in the tiny ward. She patted our hands, softly told us she was sorry for what she had done, asked our forgiveness, and told us to be good children, obey our father, and listen to the Lord. We never again saw her alive. Two days later she was dead.

Following that hospital visit, the Giles County sheriff took us across the street to his office in the courthouse.

He asked us, "What were you doing the day your mom had her accident? Did she say anything to you? Where was your daddy?"

"We were outside playing. We didn't see her at all. Daddy was not home," Clyde and Margaret responded.

As the youngest of the three children in that room, the only thing I remember saying was "Yes" when the sheriff asked me if I wanted an orange pop. Otherwise, I kept silent, then and for the next seventy years.

As you might imagine, despite the sheriff's declaration that it was suicide, small-town tongues wagged at church and school and family reunions. I have faint recollections during those early years after Mommie's death of rumors that Dad had something to do with it. Of course, that was not possible; he was up on the Ohio River at the Chesapeake and Ohio Railyard in Russell, Kentucky. Did he hold some responsibility? Maybe. It was true that Dad was gone most of the time, was bad to drink when he was home, and was not helpful to Mommie with us children, nor did he really have anything to do with chores around the house. She must have been overwhelmed and likely depressed. Beyond these sad realities, however, he had no actual involvement in her death.

Now, eighty-five-plus years later, my oldest grandchild, Shannon, shared with me some research about female suicides of yesteryear. Abortion, of course, in those days, was illegal and unthinkable. What was to be done with an unwanted pregnancy? There were no real answers beyond prayer and perseverance. But some women did try to abort, and one of the favored methods was to drink lye and hope. Could that have been the factual reason behind Mommie's death? An attempt to abort another pregnancy turned to tragic accident? Perhaps.

I also think back on bits of conversations about Mommie's persuasion toward fundamentalist religion. My brother Clyde told me of accompanying Mommie down the hill to a Liberty City revival—snakes were handled and the evangelist may have drunk poison as a test of faith. Maybe Mommie too drank the lye as a test of faith, a way of asking for help and healing. Of course, no one will ever know, but I have wondered. Any real knowledge of the *why* of her death died with her, and we were left to puzzle over such an unexpected deed. Whatever her reasons, her suicide was the darkest day in the life of our family.

Because of the uncertainty about her death, Nellie was not destined for a peaceful rest. When time for the burial came, it would have been logical for her to be buried next to her oldest child, George William Bruce, my brother who died the day he was born in 1913. His body lies in a family plot at the Pleasant Hill Methodist Church on Dublin Road near Pearisburg, but Mommie was not interred in that sacred ground. In those days, suicide was considered an unpardonable sin, so the good folk of Pleasant Hill Methodist would not allow her burial there. The refusal by the church remains a sensitive part of our family history. Mother and son separated even in death. Thus, her body came to be buried in the Brown Cemetery on the road between Belspring and Parrott.

I vividly recall the day Mommie's death train went to Belspring. Dad, my siblings, and I boarded the Norfolk and Western coach car at the Pearisburg/Liberty City station. Her body rode behind us in the mail car. It was only a short trip to the Belspring station where Perfater's hearse met us and carried her casket up to the Bruce house on Depot Street, the house where Dad was born and raised. By 1925, the house belonged to Dad's brother, the justice of the peace, my uncle Dick, and his wife, Aunt Maggie. My memory is like a faded photo; I picture family, friends, and pretty much all the Belspring folks gathered around country ham and fried chicken and all the sides. Because of the press of the crowd, the tables were set up outside the house and I picture handheld fans waving to keep away flies and yellow jackets. The whole scene reflected a pleasant summertime gathering.

So, there we were—with full-to-the-brim plates borrowed from the Belspring Methodist Church and glasses of iced tea and the inevitable and secretive moonshine that was supplied for the men in sorrow (women did not drink in those days), as well as those who wanted an excuse to imbibe. In that day and time, funeral wakes combined an opportunity to grieve and cry away sorrows with a celebration of some of the goodness of life.

Next morning, on burial day, the processional wound its way from Uncle Dick's house up the hill to Brown Cemetery; there we overlooked the Belspring Road winding its way through the mountain community of Parrott and the New River sparkling in the sun beyond. My older brother Clyde recalled listening to the crash of the river jacks (ancient river rocks rounded by the rolling New River) as they hit the metal casket. It was so clear to him that I came to think I also heard that sound. And I do summon a fuzzy image of our family and friends engaged in the mountain tradition of pitching dirt and rocks into the grave. I may have helped—and I hope I did—but a concrete memory of my participation has faded into the distance.

Mommie was but thirty-one years old when she was laid to rest beside Dad's brother, Andrew Clyde Bruce, who died in the Bluefield Train Yard in November 1915. It was just before Thanksgiving and Andrew was on his last shift before going home to visit his mother, Maggie, in Belspring. To save a step or two at work he took a shortcut between two moving coal cars, stumbled and was caught between them and mostly cut in two. He was only thirty years old when he was killed, and the horror of his death may have led to Grandma Maggie's end; the country folk said she died of a broken heart. Over the years I have thought it fitting that Mommie was buried next to my uncle and Grandma Maggie, neither of whom I knew.

Gone, but not forgotten is the epitaph on Nellie's tombstone. But to me she was largely forgotten—forgotten year upon year, until the passing of time and wrinkles on my face allowed me a safe distance from the unspeakable loss. All my life Mommie has been but a faint remembrance, but as the time for my own dying draws near, I dream about her far more now than when I was young. It's like her memory, her presence, has reappeared from that faraway place she had gone. Mostly I think of our happy times together: how she loved to dance with a broom in her kitchen, her loving ways and her comforting words to me and my siblings, the way she nurtured me through countless childhood attacks of pneumonia. I held on to all these memories and left the pain and loss deep down in the past.

I don't still dwell on the ache and loss, but seventy years after her death, my eldest grandson asked questions that prompted me to think on events I had largely forgotten and to come to some understanding in my old age that which eluded me in childhood and for most of my life. Now I have made peace with the past and realize that in the strange way life sometimes works, deep trouble and tragedy can become a mysterious wonder that opens a path to the future. A church hymn has helped me down that road of hope:

> "God moves in a mysterious way His wonders to perform. He plants His footsteps in the sea and rides upon the storm. Deep in unfathomable mines of never failing skill, He treasures up His bright designs and works His sovereign will."
>
> "God Moves in a Mysterious Way,"
> William Cowper, 1774

The events that led me to live in Belspring were truly terrible, the worst of my life. Yet growing up in that village was as good a thing as ever happened to me and my coming of age in Belspring was a great turning point in my life.

Here in life's late afternoon, there are many things I do not understand, but I have come to trust that *God does move in a mysterious way His wonders to perform.* Now, fully aware of my own mortality, I trust that some glad morning when my life is over, I will see Mommie and the "great cloud of witnesses" in Heaven.[2] We sang of such in my childhood:

> *"When we all get to Heaven, what a day of rejoicing that will be."*
>
> Eliza E. Hewitt, "When We All Get to Heaven"

---

[2] Hebrews 12:1

CHAPTER 2

Early Childhood Recollections: Coal Camps & Railyards

In the spring of my eighty-third year, my eldest son, his daughter, and a cousin or two went to southern West Virginia in search of the places and stories of my childhood and my place of birth. My early childhood centered around the coal camps and railroad yards of Virginia and West Virginia. Since Dad worked for the Norfolk and Western Railway and its chief business was hauling coal, the Bruce clan followed the coal cars. I was born in one of those camps—the McDowell County coal camp of Keystone, West Virginia in March 1917.

I WAS BORN IN A COAL CAMP. In the years in and around my birth year, coal camps were like gold rush towns. Black-gold camps had young men, new money, plenty of booze, and rampant red-light houses. Keystone had all that in abundance, plus a goodly measure of old-fashioned greed and corruption and crime. The booze came from stills along the mountain creeks; the red-light girls came in on trains from the upper south and Ohio and Pennsylvania. Their numbers were also increased by a fair-sized sprinkling of poor mountain girls who needed money. The simple reality of a town like Keystone was it provided a place where the coal miners and train men could spend their money and have a diversion from hard work—a perfect storm for debauchery and lawlessness.

More than a few drunken men in search of a lady of the night lost wallets—and in some cases, their lives—along the creeks and railway beds of Keystone. Men walking and hoboing into Cinder Bottom, the name of the red-light district in Keystone, counted themselves lucky to make it past the railway curve of Dead Man's Cut without loss of their money or their necks. I heard tell that if a coal miner or trainman was robbed and killed in Keystone, the body was tossed onto the tracks to be mutilated beyond identity by the continuous flow of railway cars. It was a hard, dangerous place.

Howard Lee, a former attorney general of West Virginia, once called Keystone the Sodom and Gomorrah of McDowell County: *"Rich in coal and railway cars and houses of ill repute, Keystone was known far and wide as the 'International Whorehouse District of the Coal Fields.'"*

When I was a younger man, I sometimes took perverse pleasure in claiming Keystone as my birthplace, since it was known as the toughest of the country's tough spots. Well into the 1950s and '60s, high school boys in the mountains of Virginia and West Virginia talked of Keystone as the place to lose their virginity. In reality, I was a toddler in Keystone, so it was tongue-in-cheek humor for me—and besides, no one now alive has any recollection of Keystone in the early 1900s.

Old photos of Keystone show a hopping main street with cars and storefronts and plenty of people. That was once upon a time, but by the year of our visit in 2000, it was a wreck of empty buildings and ruined foundations. Where once stood active, busy, occupied structures, we found it to be a black-dust blight on the world. As I looked up at the steep blackened hills surrounding the railyard, I imagined Mommie trying to keep our little hillside house and her brood of three children somewhat clean. Of course, that was not possible—millions of tons of coal and dust tumbled through that godforsaken town and left its dark mark on everyone and everything.

The only people we saw that spring day seemed broken by the harshness and poverty of life. No more than a half a dozen people were on the streets, though two or three times, from a second-story window over an old store, aging folks peered through parted curtains to watch us make our way down the block. Our car was too clean, our clothes too spiffy. We were people from a different world and time, alien to the very place I was born. Looming over the town was a huge, high and lifted-up coal chute. It was a symbol of what had been the town's life's blood, yet also its ruination. A vision of Hell on Earth—a town destroyed by the misery generated from the coal production itself and the accompanying corruption and money. That memory has stuck with me.

When I was less than a year old, our family left rugged Keystone and moved to Bluefield, Virginia/West Virginia because Dad was promoted to a freight train conductor out of the Norfolk and Western Bluefield yard. It meant we had more money, a nicer house, and closer contact with Dad's older brother, Leonard Wilson Bruce, who also lived in Bluefield. He was called "Uncle Bob" for reasons I have never known, though I have carried his middle name of Wilson all my years. Since we all lived in Bluefield, the story was told again and again at family gatherings how Uncle Andrew was crushed between two coal cars in the Bluefield yard. It became family legend for us and though we did not know him, he was a sundered hero.

While we lived in Bluefield, several days each week Dad's assignment took him on the Pond Mill Run from Bluefield through the West Virginia/Kentucky territory of the notorious Hatfields and McCoys. Those stories, too, became part of our family legend. Since Dad's train went through feud terrain, Uncle Bob suggested that Dad carry three essentials on his runs: a loaded pistol, several sandwiches (preferably baloney and cheese with mustard), and a pint of moonshine in case things got either too boring or too exciting. According to Uncle Bob, whiskey would work wonders for either of those conditions. Obviously, Dad was in his own way a rough, hard-drinking fellow and definitely not a Boy Scout, so he was prepared for the Pond Mill Runs. Clyde and I liked to imagine Dad as a gun-slinging hero, afraid of neither Hatfield nor McCoy. In reality, he never fired his pistol nor saw a real, live, honest-to-God-Hatfield or McCoy, but had he done so, he was ready for them. We carried the dream and hope that Dad would do his part to vanquish evil and bring justice to the coal fields.

What Dad did do regularly on his runs was drink his moonshine, and this constant predilection to drinking whiskey led to the loss of his job. A drink or two while on duty out of Bluefield led to a nap in the caboose, where Inspector Mitchell, no friend of Dad's, found him asleep and fired him on the spot: "George Bruce, you sorry good for nothing S.O.B., you're fired and I'm going to make certain you will never again work for the N&W Railway."

Mitchell carried through on his promise. Thus was the end of our good life in Bluefield, the curtain closing on the easy money in the coal fields of Virginia and West Virginia, and the permanent end of Dad's work on the N&W. Dad, in good mountain tradition, never forgave Mitchell and cursed him for the remainder of his natural life. "May he fry in Hell" was his lifelong hope and benediction for the inspector.

"Oh, you can't get to Heaven with a bottle of gin, 'cause the Lord, He don't let no drunkards in."

"You Can't Get to Heaven,"
Sunday School song from the days of Prohibition

Now with a jobless dad, our life in the coal camps came to a halt. We were forced to move to Pearisburg, Virginia to live in a rented house owned by Mommie's brother, French Rowe. It was a move Dad never wanted, but he had no choice.

CHAPTER 3

Pearisburg Memories:
The Calm Before the Storm

With a jobless dad and no money for a home after his dismissal from the N&W, we packed up our meager belongings and moved to the small Giles County town of Pearisburg, not far from the farm community of Pleasant Hill, which was home for Mommie's folks, the Rowes. I was five years old.

PEARISBURG was my first well-remembered home and it was a beautiful place to live, nestled alongside the New River and below Angel's Rest Overlook in the mountains. As folks who walk the Appalachian Trail know, Angel's Rest is now a favored hiking place.

Giles County and Pearisburg were home base for Mommie's family, the Rowes. Grandpa William Rowe farmed some acreage in Pleasant Hill, just outside Pearisburg on the road toward Dublin; Nellie, her sister Lois, and her brother French grew up on that farm. We never knew Grandma Louisa—she died in 1907—so to me she was just a marker in the Pleasant Hill Cemetery. In my young, childlike memory, the Pleasant Hill farm was a happy place for us. Mommie laughed frequently around her father and her siblings. Her father adored her and thought her unusually smart for a girl, although I don't think anyone in her family ever forgave Dad for eloping with her.

I have pleasing memories of the steep, rocky beauty of the Rowe land; it was a good place for a boy to visit and dream. Especially, I recall with great fondness that Grandpa Rowe took Clyde and me on long walks from the farm to the Pleasant Hill post office and store. On the walks, we all threw rocks at fence posts, but already Clyde was a dead-eye shot and won our contests, even besting Grandpa. At the store next to the post office, he bought us penny candy—my favorite was horehound. All my life, it has symbolized the taste of childhood.

Mommie's brother, French, also lived in the area and owned various rental houses. For our first year in Pearisburg, we lived in one of Uncle French's houses, a two-story wood-framed bungalow up the hill from Jockey Street, which was the monthly gathering place for trade days on spring and summer Saturdays. Every imaginable thing was for sale or barter on the street: horses, chickens, goats, fruits, vegetables, quilts, and other handmade goods. Those were special days for me; I have a distant recollection that Mommie fixed homemade peach ice cream and sold it to folks on Jockey Street for five cents; she spooned the cream into her small bowls with her kitchen spoons as utensils. The children's task was to be sure the bowls and spoons were returned to the ice cream table. If need be, we followed people who happened to walk away while eating the ice cream. When they finished, we carried the bowls and spoons back to our house, washed them, and brought them back outside to be reused. Important work for happy children.

In time, we moved to a nicer house also owned by Uncle French; it was close to the fairgrounds where the annual Giles County Fair was held. Clyde ran errands for folks; his services were in high demand and he earned a whopping nickel or dime from people made generous by the atmosphere of the fair. We sat on the stone wall at the fairgrounds on hot summer days and took in the sights of horses and pigs, pickles and preserves, wagons and the occasional car. With his few coins, a boy's treasure trove, he might buy a couple of peach ice cream cones and present one to me and we licked away and wondered if there were any boys luckier than the two of us. No ice cream ever tasted better than that. If not ice cream, it was cotton candy or caramel corn. On rare occasions, we used our riches to see a movie at the downtown Paris Cinema. Such memories linger. We were big shots for sure.

Life was good. Even school was good—in my second year, that is. During first grade, a bout of pneumonia kept me out for weeks and when I went back, I cried and cried for Mommie. My teacher was not happy with my outbursts and asked Mommie to take me home and try again the next year when I was older and healthier. In those weeks I spent home from school, Mommie worked with me on spelling until I became good at it; I still am a good speller. She also taught me to love stories and books, which I continue to do even now. Though Dad had little use for book learning, Mommie wanted us to get an education and was determined for that to happen. I reflected on this when in 1934 I graduated from Belspring School and thought how proud Mommie would be of me for that accomplishment. To finish all eleven grades and even be commended by the teachers for a scholarship to William and Mary! That was a Mommie-Nellie kind of dream, even though college was impossible for me as an orphan child. My tuition may have been paid, but I couldn't afford a place to live.

In those easy times in Pearisburg, I didn't think about or even recognize any problems in our family. To me, in that dreamy childhood way, life was just fine. In daylight hours, we went to school, came home to supper and played with our friends in vacant lots and alongside creeks. In twilight, it was "kick the can" and a race to see who could catch the most lightning bugs. Often Mommie read us a night-time story and listened to our prayers of *"now I lay me down to sleep."* Though I have no concrete recollection of it, I am sure she potty-trained us and wiped our bloodied noses and made certain we took a bath at least once a week. In the mornings, she fixed our biscuits and sausage gravy, and on special days we drank hot cocoa.

Giles County, of which Pearisburg was the county seat, mostly had an idyllic quality to it. Dad was rarely around, but that was not unusual for trainmen. In truth, I think Dad often stayed away from home because Uncle French was no fan of Dad. He thought Dad a no-count winebibber who had stolen Nellie away from her family, so family relations with the Rowes depended entirely on Mommie. Naturally Dad resented the dependence he had on Uncle French's largesse. So, in a mixture of necessity and relief, Dad concentrated on his job with the Chesapeake and Ohio Railroad up north on the Ohio River. We saw him only occasionally.

From time to time Dad did show up, however. Memories of such a time still abide with me. One weekend he drove into Pearisburg in a new, blue Hupmobile! I think the car was a way of thumbing his nose at Uncle French and everyone else who thought him a loser. On this trip down from the Ohio River, Dad had a driver—a complete necessity since Dad had a new car but had not yet learned to drive. Of course, both driver and Dad were higher than kites when they rolled into Pearisburg. All of us kids were excited to no end, but Mommie and her sister, Aunt Lois Rowe, were considerably less so.

After a supper of green beans and fat back and fried onions and potatoes with corn bread (usual fare for us), Dad's friend asked to borrow the car to escape the turmoil in the house. Off he went in Dad's new car, but Dad, whose heart was with his drunken friend, stayed with the family. After a few more nips off his bottle, Dad began to argue with Mommie and Aunt Lois. He was inebriated enough that he thought it would be great fun to chase Aunt Lois and Mommie around the house, which he proceeded to do, all the while firing his Hatfield and McCoy pistol into the ground. The fun ended when the ammunition ran out. Aunt Lois never again gave Dad the benefit of any doubt. When she died, as a nurse of some means in Roanoke, Virginia, she made clear what she thought of anyone connected with George Bruce: She willed both Clyde and me one dollar.

We arose that Saturday morning to the news that Dad's driver friend, in a drunken stupor, had hit a tree and killed himself. To say the least, it was a memorable weekend for us. Who could forget? I think, however, Dad wished we would. No more friend. No more blue Hupmobile. No more goodwill at the breakfast table. On Sunday, Dad caught a train and headed back to northern Kentucky with head and shoulders down, like a whipped cur dog. We never again heard of the Hup nor where Dad's dead driver friend may have been buried. Dad never again came into Pearisburg as a big man around town.

"Those were the days, my friend, we thought they'd never end."
"Those Were the Days," Boris Fomin &
Gene Raskin, 1968

As I remember it, Pearisburg was a good place for us and I still carry the good times in my bank of memories, but Mommie's death ended our childlike reverie and innocence. Now we knew, as all children do sooner or later, that life can be a time of hard knocks as much as it is laughter and happiness. With Mommie's death, the desolate side of life came home to us in a way that before was only rumor as from a bad dream. Now for us, pain and disappointment were a major portion of life's experience.

As I look back on those good times in Pearisburg through the lens of Mommie's sudden and horrible death, I am aware that the church, and in particular hymns of the church, have given me an optimism about my life and its future. Over the years, I sat through many tepid sermons and prayers that instructed God on what to do for us, but it was the hymns that tugged at my heart and mind and kept me coming back to church all my life. Often of a Sunday, my heart did and does ring with a melody and the hope of a fairer day.

"There's a land that is fairer than day, and by faith we can see it afar. For the Father waits over the way to prepare us a dwelling place there."
"There is a Land that is Fairer than Day,"
Sandford Bennett, 1868

"In my heart there rings a melody, there rings a melody with Heaven's harmony."

"In My Heart There Rings a Melody,"
Elton M. Roth, 1924

CHAPTER 4

Our Dad – George Cleveland Bruce

Many in Belspring knew Dad by his nickname, Brownie. Like the good-natured elf from Scottish lore, Brownie/Dad was known in our town as one to make folks laugh. His buddies liked to have his smiling face around when moonshine was plentiful and laughter was needed. As the baby in his family, he was spoiled by his momma and his older brothers and in some ways, people kept on spoiling him all his life. If he could be the center of attention, he was willing to be the jokester in a crowd. It was a role he played, and relished, all his days.

FOR THOSE OF MY GENERATION, the words in Exodus about honoring parents came as close as any of us knew to the actual words of God Almighty. We could cite the other nine commandments as well, but this one was a daily experience, either to be observed in regular duty or broken with guilt in its trail. So, in spite of the fragmentation of our family, we honored and loved a Mommie who had abruptly and finally left us. It was the same with our dad, George, or Brownie. We knew of Dad's many foibles, but he was our dad and we honored and loved him until he died.

"Honor thy father and thy mother that thy days may be long."
Exodus 20

Simply put, Dad was a character and my loving remembrance of him needs to honor that. For one thing, he was a member of Belspring's largest male club: the booze-hounds. For much of his life, he was in pursuit of a good, stiff drink—it was a rare Belspring man who wasn't engaged in this pursuit. He was well-trained to cherish whiskey; all the male population of Belspring, including his older brothers, were mentors. This background prepared him for his first real job when he left home to work on the railroad with the Norfolk & Western Railway. Most of the men of the N&W were drinkers and Dad fit right in. He continued the tradition over his work career, which also included his time with the Chesapeake and Ohio after he was fired from the N&W.

Like most railroad men, Dad was out of work in the Depression. He was single, all his children somewhat settled elsewhere, so he came back to Belspring from Ohio and rented a small house behind Calhoun's Store. He shared it with his out-of-work buddy, Jimmy Burnette. Bored, jobless, they tried the hobo life, which may have been inspired by a hobo camp near Blacksburg, Virginia. Tales around the campfire at night kindled a desire to hit the rails, and that they did. Caught a freight coming through Belspring; it was already populated by men on the move. Up into West Virginia and Ohio and Michigan they rode the rails, working a little and begging a lot. By Thanksgiving, they were in a little town outside Detroit; hungry, they knocked on the door of a farmhouse and a kindly lady gave then each a turkey leg.

When Dad recounted the turkey leg story, he told me with tears in his eyes, "Made me realize there are still some good people in the world." And those good people here and there kept them going until they arrived in

Minnesota in the dead of winter in a snowstorm. The temperature dropped fast and well below zero. He and his pal, Jimmy, and a couple of other guys were in a boxcar. Fearful of freezing to death during the night, they tore the siding off the inside walls and started a fire in the middle of the car to make enough warmth to survive the night. Next morning, they hopped a freight train headed south.

Days later they jumped off a freight in Belspring. Dad, sick as a dog, was leaning on Jimmy as they hobbled up Depot Street to their bungalow. Dad's hoboing days were over, but his half-baked ideas yet had root in his brain.

Being a bootlegger was one of those ideas. Several men around Belspring and Parrott were successful at selling the "shine" that kept menfolk temporarily happy, so Dad and Jimmy figured they could do it too. Since they had no vehicle and were averse to much walking, they hopped a freight car in Belspring and made their way to Vicker Switch near Christiansburg and purchased two gallons of moonshine from a well-known whiskey maker. Treasure in hand, they freight-trained it back to Belspring and set up shop. Word went out that Brownie and Jimmy had whiskey to sell. Male friends knocked on the door, one bought a pint on credit. Of course, everyone sampled; soon the house was full of roaring drunks.

The next morning, a Saturday, I walked up to check on Dad: drunks were passed out on the floor, on the steps, and on every other available space. Even Uncle Dick came and told Dad, "Brownie, half the ladies in Belspring have complained to me about the swearing and drinking and noise. You have to get this house in order or I'll be forced to call the law from Pulaski." It was the sad end of the great Belspring whiskey business. They made no profit and never so much as received the money on the pint taken on credit. All those guys are long dead, but their two-gallon-drunk story lived on as long as they breathed.

I also celebrate the stories my older sister, Margaret, passed on to me—of how Dad romanced Mommie with love notes in a crack in the big rock near the rail tracks where they had first seen one another; then in a scene as if from an old movie, they eloped. Caught a train and went to Bristol, Tennessee and for a long time they were happy. Job and money issues and the strains of life made for hard times and then Mommie was gone and nothing was ever the same. I think Dad coped as best he knew how and all five of us children stayed close to him until he died in 1967 at age seventy-nine.

And there are other Dad stories worth retelling and remembering. At Christmastime about 1945, Rosie and I and our oldest child went to Toledo to see Dad and his third wife, Ethel. Dad had scoped out a good place where the railroad guys went to drink. Off the two of us went over snowy, icy roads to find the two-for-one special drinks. Found it we did, and we drank enough to make the railroad proud and then wove our way through the downtown Toledo streets with sparks from my dragging tailpipe marking our departure.

Safe at Brownie and Ethel's old, two-story apartment near the C&O Railyard and Toledo's Union Station, Ethel proceeded to chastise Brownie, whereupon Dad, decked out in his shoes, socks, suit with vest, and his homburg hat, climbed into the bathtub and threatened to turn on the water. Ethel calmly walked to the faucet and said matter-of-factly, "Here, George, let me help you turn on the water." His bluff called, Dad stumbled out of the tub. Ethel, a Belspring girl, was not a woman with whom to trifle.

One more Brownie story. In 1963, my oldest boy married in the Fairlawn Methodist Church. Dad attended with my older sister, Margaret. Midway through the service, Dad started crying. When the service ended Margaret asked him what he was crying about. His reply: "I kept seeing myself up in front of that church laying in a casket." I treasure that story, for except for an occasional funeral, Dad did not darken church doors. He did not want to hear messages about the evils of drink or chasing women, or the need to give money, so he did not go. But he was concerned about being dead as a doornail and laying in a casket.

Even though his later years were spent up in Toledo, or in Covington, Virginia so he could be near the C&O Hospital and doctors, Belspring was always his home and I went to see him often and even named my youngest boy George. I remained proud to call him Dad, or any of the names by which he was known.

CHAPTER 5

A Trek into the Wilderness
Russell & Ironton

In 1925–26, the reality of life for my family was this: Mommie was dead and buried in the Brown Cemetery in Belspring; Dad was in Russell, Kentucky working in the huge C&O railyard along the Ohio River; my brothers and sisters and I were in Belspring and Parrott and Pleasant Hill and Narrows—separated in five different homes. We were as dispersed as the ancient Israelites and trouble always seemed near at hand.

SCATTERED AS WE ALL WERE with Margaret, Hazel, and I in and around Belspring, Clyde at Grandpa Rowe's in Pleasant Hill, Jimmy on Wolf Creek out from Narrows, and Dad working far away out of Kentucky and Ohio, the responsibility for the Bruce children increasingly fell to Dad's older brother, Dick Bruce. But Uncle Dick, Belspring's justice of the peace, had his own job and family, so watching over our brood was a burden for him. The straw that broke Uncle Dick's back was when my brother Clyde got in trouble one more time—this particular instance involved beating up on Grandpa Rowe's stepson. Thus, Uncle Dick's call to Dad: "Brownie, you have to come to Belspring and do something about your children."

So, as soon as was possible, Dad came to Belspring with a plan. Hazel and Jimmy—who by this time had been brought from Wolf Creek to Parrott—were to stay in Belspring while the three oldest of our brood (Margaret, Clyde, and me) were to go to Russell, Kentucky to live with Dad and our new mother, along with her three children. I don't believe she and Dad ever married—not that this made much difference for people as rambling as we were. The reason for this arrangement was simple: Dad needed a woman to care for his children; she needed a man with a paycheck. It was a match made in Hades. Our new mother, Mildred, and her three kids of more or less the same age as us, were a perfect target for our own thinly disguised anger at our situation in life.

The arrangement never had a real chance. No one, especially New Mother, could tell Margaret or Clyde anything; they had too much hostility at the world because of Mommie's death and I took my cue from them. The situation was a setup for failure. Dad worked at night and slept in the day; Mildred's charge was to keep the house clean and quiet and keep the children out of his room when he was asleep. Of course, that wasn't possible. I came up with a good plan to take advantage of this situation. Since New Mother's boy of my age and I fought all the time, and since he was bigger and stronger than me, I needed a strategy. My plan was to get in my licks early and then run to Dad's bedroom for safety. It worked well, until my opponent sailed a tin can lid at me. It caught me on the wrist; I bled like a stuck hog. The general hubbub and my bloody arm had the house in an uproar that ended with Dad spanking both me and my foe. All these eighty years later, I still carry the wrist scar of his good shot. It wasn't long until Mildred and her three children boarded a train and went back to West Virginia. Dad took us three across the Ohio River and rented a different house in the big town of Ironton, Ohio; probably ten thousand folks living there.

Dad spelled out our responsibilities: Margaret was to cook and be housekeeper; Clyde and I were to go to school. Obviously, Margaret had the rough edge of that stick; it was hard to be a girl, then and now. We all more or less kept to a plan that was doomed from the beginning. Margaret worked hard, and she and Dad argued most days about the unfairness of it all. Clyde and I went to school, except the times we played hooky and walked downtown to the newspaper office to watch its building-side mock-up of the Cincinnati Reds game. A baseball diamond was outlined on the side of the building and a loudspeaker broadcast the game as a lighted dot showed the position of any hit or base runner. The whole town turned out on ballgame nights and Clyde and I were part of the crowd. It was an astonishment, light years away from Belspring. I still dream of that diamond and those games.

> *"Take me out to the ball game…buy me some peanuts and cracker jacks. I don't care if I never get back."*
> 1908 song – "Tin Pan Alley"
> by Jack Norworth and Albert Von Tilze

School days were mostly forgettable, but they did have their memorable times, like the teacher who gave a paddling to the boys when we misspelled words on Friday's spelling bee. Girls never got a spanking; I couldn't figure out if they just spelled all the words correctly or if the teacher had it in for the boys. Thanks to Mommie, I was a good speller, but I was so intimidated by that teacher and her paddle, I couldn't spell anything right; words and letters would not come out of my mouth. So, you could write it in your book that I received a paddling every Friday and also gained a reputation as a birdbrain and retard. The other boys called Clyde and me "dumb mountaineers."

Revenge is sweet, and we got a portion of it on a Saturday walk in the woods. Clyde and I happened onto a gathering of some of our tormentors up in a tree house. We heard and saw them before we were seen, and we hatched an ambush: we collected a big pile of rocks and on signal cut down on them in their tree haven. I could throw fair, but Clyde launched a wicked rock; there were some knots and bruises on our tormentors from his missiles. When a rock struck home, we laughed though they showered us with the promise that we would be sorry we were ever born. No one ventured out of that tree, but eventually our pile of rocks ran out and we hightailed it. Clyde likely would have made it home, but I was slower, and he would not leave me, so we were captured and beat around a bit. They stripped us naked and made us walk home with nothing on but our birthday suits. We hid behind as many bushes as we could find, but quite a number of folks saw our skinny behinds that Saturday.

Clyde's refusal to run and leave me behind to my own fate sealed for me the truth that he was my blood brother. As long as he was alive and by my side, I was going to be okay.

At home we received what we anticipated—Dad's belt on our bottoms—but it was pretty gentle. He was proud of the fact that it took seven Yankee boys from Ohio to subdue two young mountaineers from Virginia. We were fairly tough on that day, regardless of the nudity on the streets of Ironton, and I still chuckle at the thoughts of it.

It wasn't long until Dad gave up on the Russell/Ironton experiment. It was time to go on home to Belspring and our kind of folks.

"I'm on my way to Canaan land...I've asked my brother and sister to come with me. Praise God, I'm on my way."

An old slave spiritual

CHAPTER 6

Home Is a Village, Farm, Cemetery

By varying routes, we wound our way down the road to Belspring:
Mommie first in the cold, hard ground of Brown Cemetery, but Dad, me,
my brothers and sisters followed to this place that was to be home.
Through times both good and bad, the village and the land kept us united.
Our heart's place in the Earth was the Belspring of our childhood.

AS I THINK BACK ON OUR CHILDHOOD, I realize that the times were hardest for young Jimmy and, as is so often true, for the two girls, Margaret and Hazel. To my way of thinking, Clyde and I had it easier.

Jimmy, two when Mommie died, first went from Pearisburg to live with some of her kin in the wild mountain country near Wolf Creek outside Narrows, Virginia. Wolves prowled the mountains in those days, at least according to popular lore, so in the middle of that wilderness world, Jimmy—a big boy for his age—largely had to fend for himself among those ridges and hollows. Word filtered back to Uncle Dick that he was neglected, so Uncle's Model T went from Belspring to Wolf Creek where he found a neglected, scratched and bruised urchin.

Having anticipated the worst, Uncle went with the knowledge that he needed to fetch Jimmy back to the Bruce home on Depot Street. The only trouble with that scenario was that Dick and Maggie's home was already crowded with rambunctious boys and though Aunt Maggie loved Jimmy, she did not want another child in the house. Uncle Dick then made arrangements for Jimmy to stay temporarily with Lottie and Ford Hamilton on a farm overlooking the Belspring Road with views of nearby Parrott Mountain while Dad made other plans for him. Temporary soon became permanent because Dad had no way to keep Jimmy with him. Thus, little brother was practically a Hamilton. That changed on a fateful day when Ford was on his property at work in his truck mine (a small coal mine named for the hand- or horse-pulled wagon that brought the coal out of the mine). As he slammed his pick into a coal seam, it collapsed, and rock and coal buried him. Lottie sent Jimmy to call Ford to supper and Jimmy found him interred beneath rock and coal. For a young boy, it seemed as if trouble lurked around every corner or in every mine shaft.

Unable to work the farm solo, Lottie soon married Fult Lindsey, who became Jimmy's new poppa, or Uncle Fult as Jimmy called him. It remained this way until Jimmy finally left to join the Air Force. At sixteen, before he left home for good, Jimmy ran away as boys will do—I don't remember exactly why. He jumped a freight train down on the N&W rails and made it all seven miles to the Radford railyard only to be arrested by a rail detective and jailed as a vagrant. He served time in the Radford jail and was assigned street cleanup duty under an armed guard. A Belspring/Parrott man saw him at work on a Radford street; Fult was informed and bailed him out. Fult, who was tighter than the bark on a tree about money, wanted to leave Jimmy in jail, but Lottie prevailed and for the sake of peace in the family, Fult sprung him. I doubt that Jimmy, even after he married and moved to Fort Worth, Texas, ever heard the end of Fult's opinion about it all.

Jimmy was a funny boy and man, full of goodness and bluster and tall stories. I still laugh when I think about him and his break for freedom, making it all the way from Belspring to Radford. And I laugh, too, about one of Jimmy's visits from Texas when we were fifty and older. We ventured to Bland County accompanied by a distant cousin, Old Man Bill Bruce (William Amos). Jimmy kept the air warm with his stories. Old Man Bill came to see me about a week later; one of his comments was "that brother of yours is a mite windy." Yes, he was, and more than a mite of a brother—the biggest one of us all.

Sister Hazel went from Pearisburg straight to Belspring—taken in by the Caldwell's childless son, Bob, and his wife Mae Linkous Caldwell. They lived in a small house right behind Fanny and Doley and me. Not more than a hundred feet or so up the hill, Hazel and I thought ourselves the most fortunate of children. We saw each other daily and went to school and church together where we giggled our way through the long and boring Methodist prayers. Uncle Bob Caldwell was one of the wordier folks as he prayed both God and congregation into submission; when he wasn't the chief pray-er, he was handy with a loud "Amen." In preparation for those Methodist Sundays, Fanny and Mae scrubbed our faces until they had a cherubic shine and Mae sewed up some of her best cloth for her little girl.

On one level it was the best of times for Hazel and me: backyard picnics, jaunts down to the Depot to watch a passenger train zip by; baptisms witnessed by the pool on Back Creek; fried chicken and apple pie on Sundays. On school nights, we tested one another in spelling and reading. At night we chased a million fireflies, or so it seemed; we were very close. Brother and sister: "She ain't heavy, she's my sister."

There were other times when I realized Hazel was down, as if a dark cloud followed her. I never knew the cause of that darkness. Likely, Mommie's death played a large part. Much later in her life, Hazel went into a deep depression from which she only recovered in fits and spurts. Word from the Belspring alleys was that as a child, she may have been abused. I never knew the facts of the matter, nor did I talk about it until long after Uncle Bob and Aunt Mae and Hazel and Doley and Fanny were dead, but maybe, just maybe, there was some truth to it. When I look back over our lives, I realize that the effects of Mommie's death went on, in unspoken and hidden ways, long years after her burial. And whatever the real story, sweet and pretty Hazel carried a heavy burden to her own grave.

"As I went down in the river to pray, studying about that good ol' way and who shall wear the starry crown? Good Lord show me the way. Oh sister, let's go down, let's go down, won't you come on down. Oh, sister, let's go down, down in the river to pray."

Traditional Appalachian song

Margaret was thirteen when Mommie died. She was the closest to Nellie; they were almost like older and younger sister. Thirteen years old and your best friend and Mother dies by her own hand. It's no wonder Margaret was an alcoholic by the time she was twenty. For a stretch when she first came to Belspring, she made her own way by keeping house, cleaning, and cooking for folks. She received mixed reviews, for Margaret did not like anyone telling her what to do. If they tried it, she might well give them a piece of her mind. Her pay was usually board and meals and not much else. In time, she was known to dip into a family man's booze supply; she liked drink as much as any man, but of course, it was a day and time when women were not allowed to drink. Besides, it was the days of the temperance movement.

Margaret's keep was partly solved when Dad's job disappeared, and he moved into the little house behind Calhoun's Store. Dad, Margaret, and Clyde lived there together and at times sparks flew. Once, at wit's end, Margaret was ironing shirts with one of those old cast-iron irons; she and Clyde argued, and she reared back and fired the iron at Clyde's head. It was a close miss. Thereafter Clyde stepped a little livelier around Margaret.

Through thick and thin and a long hospitalization for alcoholism, Margaret came out on the other end of matters as a head nurse at various hospitals in West Virginia and Ohio. She was the only one of us who had any education beyond public school; she was married three times, never having any children, and spent most of her adult life living near her younger sister, Hazel, in Perrysburg, Ohio. She was like a second momma to Hazel's three children.

"For the wonder of each hour, of the day and of the night … for the mystic harmony, linking sense to sound and sight, Lord of all, to Thee we raise this our hymn of grateful praise."

"For the Beauty of the Earth,"
Folliott Pierpont hymn, 1864

CHAPTER 7

My Hero Clyde Cleveland Bruce

My older brother, Clyde Cleveland Bruce, died in 2004 at age eighty-nine. I was eighty-seven at that time and I confess I have missed him in a way that I would not have thought. Clyde was the last tie to my family of origin and his death shook me to my core.

"Behold, how good and pleasant it is, when brothers dwell together in unity…there the Lord commanded the blessing, even life forevermore."

Psalm 133

I WAS NOT PREPARED for how deeply Clyde's death would affect me. After all, the rest of my family of origin was gone by that time and Clyde and I were very old men; in that sense, were just marking time until we too, would pass over the river. But knowing this did not spare me the long weeks of sadness or the depth of my feeling about his absence. Now, in hindsight, I realize it was only natural that I would miss him sorely. I still do and I'm glad I do; it makes his life all the more precious.

Clyde, by two years my elder brother, was my childhood hero, the one who more than anyone else watched over the small, sickly child that I was. Before Mommie's death, Clyde and I were close in that special way that connects big brothers to little brothers. He was both fraternal and paternal, as Dad was seldom around. Bigger, stronger, and faster than me, even when we were quite young, he could throw a ball or rock with amazing accuracy and speed. Boys, in particular, understand the imaginative power of a well-thrown rock. This skill meant that older boys, if sometimes tempted to pick on me, waned in his presence.

He also did some extra things that live on in my memory with gratitude. For instance, in those Pearisburg days, we lived close to Jockey Street, a trade street for farmers and merchants where everything from a pig to a popsicle was for sale or trade. Older folks in the crowd learned that eight-year-old Clyde was a dependable errand boy. For only pennies in tips, Clyde would skedaddle to a sandwich stand and fetch a hot dog or barbecue sandwich. I usually received a small portion of the tips I had not earned.

When we had to leave Pearisburg, Clyde's life was not easy. First, he stayed with Mommie's poppa, William Rowe, but that did not last long. New Grandma's son and Clyde mixed like oil and water. They were often in a tussle and while Clyde may have won the battle, he lost the war—New Grandma wanted Clyde out of the house. Next, there was a brief time he spent with a family named Bays up on Parrott Mountain. Mrs. Bays decided Clyde needed a switching, but Clyde would not cooperate and again Uncle Dick had to intervene. This meant that when he was as young as ten, he was pretty much on his own or living in Dad's rented shack behind Calhoun's Store.

By the time he was fifteen, Clyde went with Dad to work on the Maryland Conowingo Dam and he saved enough money to buy an old Oakland Sports Cabriolet car (a forerunner to the Pontiac; the Oakland was discontinued in 1931). The Cabriolet had futuristic features like the electric horn and an automated windshield cleaner. He was very proud of that car and the exciting life it would enable him to experience. After the Conowingo Dam project ended, Clyde drove the car with Dad to Belspring. Opportunity and adventure awaited.

One such occasion occurred when Clyde and his buddy, Charlie Linkous, were out and about in Belspring and Parrot and bought some whiskey. They came home at least *three sheets to the wind* and told Dad (Brownie) that they were going out for another spin. Dad told them they were not.

An argument ensued, and Clyde told Dad that it was his car, bought with his money, and he was going for another ride. Dad responded by calmly cold-clocking his oldest boy with a quick right to the chin. Clyde was laid out on the floor while the excitable, inebriated Charlie went running down the alley to his sister, Mae Caldwell and burst into the house saying: "O Mae, it's awful. Brownie's done killed Clyde." Fortunately, Clyde lived on, but he didn't drive that night and nursed a sore jaw instead.

I loved Clyde in part because he did things of which I only fantasized. In the early 1930s, there were no jobs to be had by a young man needing gas money, yet running whiskey was a prosperous vocation for anyone with a car. The errand boy had morphed into a hot driving bootlegger who delivered moonshine throughout the Belspring/Parrott end of the county. The product spread—as did Clyde's reputation—and new runs soon became available. However, the law in Pulaski heard he was going to make a whiskey run down Hickman Cemetery Road to Belspring and a roadblock was made ready. Clyde and his partner Charlie saw the feds waiting; Clyde swerved the Cabriolet through a fence and into a pasture where they made their getaway through scattering cows. He and Charlie tossed the contraband bottles into a pond with plans to return and fish them out later. Sans the booze, they eventually got into Belspring ahead of the law. Uncle Dick hid the car in a local alley garage and told the inquiring Pulaski lawmen that no one had come into town. Clyde was our very own whiskey runner.

That night Uncle Dick came to Dad and told him that the car had to go, or Clyde was bound for arrest, jail, and likely prison, since the feds were involved. The next day Clyde went to school; while he was gone, Dad sold the car for $50 with instructions to get it out of the county immediately. That afternoon when he returned from school, Clyde looked for his pride and joy—and found no car.

He said to Dad, "How could you sell my car? It wasn't yours."

Dad's reply: "Well, I sold it, and that's that. No more car."

I have forgotten how exactly Clyde and Charlie retrieved the whiskey, but they did, much to the joy of the boozehounds of Belspring. In later years, Dad bought himself a car but still had not learned to drive, so he gave it to Clyde. I guess it was to make up for the car that Dad had sold all those years before to keep Clyde out of prison.

In the mid-1930s, Clyde joined the Army and left Belspring. His legendary baseball skills finally got their chance to shine and he ended up playing third base for the Army team in Hawaii. When his hitch was up about 1938, the Army tried to get him to sign on again so he could continue playing ball, but he'd had enough of Hawaii; he headed homeward to marry his Parrott sweetheart, Josephine Giles, and start their life together.

As was his way, Clyde's timing was right; he missed the attack on Pearl Harbor.

He settled into life in Belspring and Parrott as a married man, a Methodist deacon, and church song leader. I can still picture his smiling face in front of the Methodists ready to testify and sing with a mischievous twinkle in his eye. He was now a saved man, as we were prone to say. As the Sons of the Pioneers sang it, no more "cigarettes and whiskey and wild, wild women."[3]

When we were small children in Pearisburg, Clyde and I shared a bed. After Mommie died and we lived in different places, I missed the security of my brother at night. I miss the security of him now and I anticipate that when my death beckons and the chariot swings low and carries me away, we will have a glad reunion in the sky.

"If you get to Heaven before I do, coming for to carry me home, tell all my friends I'm coming there, too, coming for to carry me home. Swing low, sweet chariot, coming for to carry me home."
American negro spiritual, 1862

---

[3] Sons of the Pioneers, "Cigarettes and Whiskey and Wild, Wild Women," 1947.

CHAPTER 8

Home at Last
Uncle Doley & Aunt Fanny

*When we left Ironton in 1926, we were bound for Belspring and
Parrott with the clear notion that it was to be a glad reunion with
Hazel and Jimmy and others we knew.
I was going home, to a people and place of the heart.*

MARGARET, CLYDE, AND I disembarked from
the train at the Belspring Depot and I felt as though I
touched sacred ground. Home. This was the land of my
grandparents, my dad, my siblings, uncles, aunts, and
cousins. Even though we owned nothing, this land was
ours—from the New River to Parrott Mountain and on
up the Belspring Road toward Highland and Radford. It
looked and smelled like the promise of a future.

The Caldwells were not blood kin, but they had been
friends of the Bruces for years; they knew my
grandparents and had watched my dad and his brothers
grow up. They knew the Belspring stories: all the
characters, their foibles, and their goodness. The
Caldwells' own children were grown, and they had house
and heart enough to take in a little Bruce boy who had
one mottled green eye and one brown (Aunt Fanny was
fascinated by my eyes). Thus began my new life on the
Belspring Road.

I loved Fanny and Doley; they were like second parents and grandparents to me. Their house faced the Belspring Road and I was installed in my own bedroom on the second floor. On the front of the house was a spacious porch; out back a sprawling garden with a proper Johnny house to one side. Fanny managed the household and worked the garden; I was her assistant. Doley had an important job at the Parrott Coal Mine as the inspector, who made certain the miners could safely occupy the mineshafts that day. Each morning, Doley walked down the Belspring Road to the River Road and on to the mine; he entered the shaft that was to be worked carrying his wick lamp with a flame enclosed inside a mesh screen. If mine-damp was present, the flame elongated, which meant that particular shaft was not safe for miners until the fans pulled out the gas. The word *mine damp* references several mining terms such as *white damp* (carbon monoxide), *fire damp* (typically methane) and *stink damp* (hydrogen sulfide). Only after a second check to confirm that the gas was no longer present could work proceed. I thought him a brave man who risked his life daily. Needless to say, he was highly respected and well paid.

After I lived with the Caldwells for a couple of years, Uncle Doley went to Radford and bought a practically new Chevrolet. He couldn't drive and never learned, so at age ten, I became his chauffeur. Before 5:00 AM daily, I drove him to the mine and then raced home at the Chevy's top speed of 35 MPH. At noon, I was excused from school, walked down the alley to the house, and drove the car to the mine to pick up Doley. Those were some of the happiest days of my life. (Can you imagine being a small boy of ten driving my uncle to and from work? Life was as good as one could hope for in those moments.) For most of the driving, I had to stand to shift gears and brake because I was too short to reach the pedals otherwise. Although pint-sized among my classmates, I was a hero to them—they could only dream of driving an auto.

Life with the Caldwells was good for me in many ways: I worked the garden with Aunt Fanny and she taught me everything I know about growing vegetables. I was in charge of burying the cabbage heads in the dirt and straw for winter use. They were buried stalk up, and in the wintertime, I had the particular joy of pulling up the cabbages, which had turned white and delicious. Anyone who has buried and dug up cabbages has been in communion with Mother Nature, and with God, too. I was also in charge of drying and turning the leather britches—green beans that we dried on the roof and then kept in bags for the winter. The britches were a wonderful excuse to be on the roof—a place for uninterrupted dreams including a daredevil climb out on the old oak limb that hung near the house. I was master of roof and sky.

In my memory bank, Christmas with the Caldwells stands out. Every year, Uncle Doley ordered a barrel of oysters from Norfolk for oyster stew and fried oysters. A pick-up Blue Grass band played in the yard, including the mine superintendent on the banjo, and folks flat-footed in the yard. Friends and neighbors and family all looked forward to Doley and Fanny's party. Fanny, in spite of being a tee-totaling Methodist, allowed beer and moonshine to be available for the menfolk, and there was plenty of tea and lemonade for the rest of us. These times were a grand celebration of a kind I had never experienced before. Then on Christmas morning, the Caldwells made sure I had a stocking filled with an orange and a peppermint stick and horehound hard candies (my favorite). In those days, children—especially half-orphans like I was—did not receive store-bought gifts. In the consumer-crazed world of today, children would not understand that, but for me it was a wonder-filled time. Even in old age, I experience butterflies thinking of Christmas morning excitement. For me, memories are made of hard candy and oranges.

Fanny and Doley were fine people. They treated others fairly and were deeply religious, especially Fanny. Every Sunday, Fanny and I, and often Doley too when he could, were in the Sunday School classrooms and after that, in the church pew at Belspring Methodist Church. I've been a churchgoer and Christian all my life and attribute much of it to Doley and especially to Fanny. They certainly top my list of church saints.

"For all the saints who from their labors rest, who Thee, by faith, before the world confessed, Thy name oh, Jesus, be forever blessed."

William Walsham How, 1864

Since Doley and Fanny could not read or write, no books were in the household; even when he bought the Chevy, all Doley could write on the contract was an X. But at age nine, I had learned to read and could interpret things for the Caldwells. Until I was grown and on my own, I owned exactly two books: the Bible, given to me by Aunt Fanny, and *The Complete Works of Shakespeare*, gifted to me by my high school English teacher, which I read from cover to cover. She thought I had real promise as a reader. Now my oldest grandson, who earned a Ph.D. in literature, has that book. Since there were no books at the Caldwells', my imagination was fed by the common, ordinary things of life: beans drying on the roof accompanied by bees and flies; white cabbages in the winter; Aunt Fanny's refusal to eat or drink anything from a store other than coffee, sugar, or flour, or her insistence that eating anything cold, including ice cream, would go straight to her heart and kill her. My delight in life was fueled by Boonie Carden's skunk cages and Shine Bland's moonshine business—all this and far more contributed to a rich building of castles in my mind and unrestricted dreams.

I've always wondered if Fanny's refusal to eat cold things had some connection to the Chinese men who came through the Belspring area building both the railroad and the Cowan Tunnel. The Chinese did not eat or drink anything cold, probably because they had no way to keep food cold, but maybe Fanny thought this made them healthy and therefore she would try it too. Makes for a good tale anyway.

Another interesting aspect of living at the Caldwells' home involved the location of my bedroom. I slept upstairs in the room next to Taft Caldwell's bedroom. Taft, the eldest son of Fanny and Doley, died in that room years before. Fanny believed he died from eating a hot cantaloupe and she would not be persuaded of any other explanation. Likely his appendix burst, and he died a painful death. However, over the years, we all witnessed irregular times when the sound of footsteps emerged from Taft's old room, walked up the hall and down the stairs. The footsteps always stopped at the door of the old kitchen. The source of the steps was always an abiding mystery to us, but the family believed it was Taft's ghost not yet at rest from his painful death. These sounds continued for years, including much later when my brother, Clyde, bought the house and moved in with his family. A few years after that, the footsteps did cease. Taft's ghost had walked himself out, I reckon.

Doley and Fanny gave me a shot at a good and joyous life; it's all anyone can hope for. They gave me a home, and nearby in Neck and Back Creeks, a place to fish and catch crawdads. In the pools of the New River, a quarter mile down Depot Street, I whiled away many an hour skipping rocks and swimming in the deep hole just below the Depot. I explored passable caves that stretched under the hills and roads and played in the old Hickman Cemetery—just me and my buddies and the dead bodies. At night, it was a hop and a jump to Parrott Mountain where my pal Hensel and I found skunks to chase in the hopes they would spray us, so we might be dismissed from school the next day because our clothes stunk to high heaven.

These tangible people and events, though decades ago, are still for me the *"precious memories, how they linger."* In my prayers, I thank God for the Caldwells who gave me a good life and through whom I entered into the household of God. I look forward to a grand reunion in the sky…and I am eager to ask Aunt Fanny if she's changed her mind about hot cantaloupe.

PART TWO

BELSPRING LIFE & COMMUNITY

*The cast of characters and places in Belspring/Parrott
that enriched my life in childhood and beyond.*

CHAPTER 9

Belspring Depot Station

There were three main destinations in the Belspring community: Calhoun's Store, the combined Buckland's Store and post office, and the Norfolk and Western Railway Station Depot. These places were the social and commercial centers of our village providing connections to each other and our dreams beyond.

I'M GLAD THAT I SPENT BOYHOOD in a village with a train depot station. It was only a simple wooden building that functioned as train stations do, but for me and countless others it was a magical spot in the earth. To our way of thinking it was almost holy ground. Not only was it the realm where our small world met a larger one, it was also for me and our family the very spot where life and death were only thinly separated; after all, the Depot was the physical locale of the train's delivery of Mommie's body. Not a one of us Bruce children would ever forget that it was here that the dismal reality of her dead body represented a holy promise fulfilled, of a life after death.

"This train is bound for glory, this train… Get on board. Get on board. Get on board this holy train."

Traditional American folk song

Though the station was torn down long ago, it has remained for me a place of memory where the spirit of childhood and family lingered next to the N&W depot. The image persists of a day during the Great Depression, when Carroll McCoy and I gathered a pile of river jacks to rock any hobo who came through on a freight train; at least that was our plan until a big, black guy had other designs. He was riding on a flatbed railcar hauling heavy machinery and Carroll and I thought him an excellent target—that is until we cocked our arms for the toss and he pulled a long, barreled pistol out of his pants and waved at us with a big grin. We hit the ground belly first while he laughed on down the rails. Hopefully, he lived on to tell the tale to his children and grandchildren, as I am doing now.

To add to the otherworldly aura of the railway and depot were the stories of the Santa train, especially during Depression days. Though generally most folks who lived on or near a farm had enough to eat, some were hungry, or needed a hope to chew on, and everyone needed coal for cooking and heating and a story of goodwill to cheer the heart. At Christmas on the Santa train railway, employees bagged coal and apples and cornmeal and one of them dressed in a Santa suit and threw off sacks near cabins and shacks. No wonder that for many of us, Santa was as good a fellow as Jesus. For years, a variation of this practice was carried on at the Belspring Methodist Church when paper sacks of nuts and hard candy and apples were distributed to everyone by a deacon dressed as Santa.

And who in Belspring did not thrill to a speeding passenger train on its way to Roanoke or Cincinnati? How fortunate could a person be to ride in such speed

and luxury? Fantasies were set in motion by these "magic carpets made of steel."

Because the Depot was such a central part of the Belspring community, it was a frequent destination for curiosity and entertainment for bored young boys. One day a guy was spraying disinfectant in the men's room of the Depot. I recall it because I had a terrible case of poison oak; sores were all over my arms and legs. He saw my itching misery: "Boy, this stuff I'm spraying will kill that poison oak and I'll squirt you up if you want. It will hurt like the mischief, but it will kill the poison." He was right; it burned like fire, so much so that I had to run around and around the Depot, but that night at the Caldwells I slept like a baby. I don't know what the stuff was, and I don't ever again want to be sprayed with it, but it worked: *Precious, painful memories, how they linger.*

The Depot and rail life were in my blood, since Dad and Uncle Bob and Uncle Andrew all grew up with engines and rail cars in their veins and one of my first jobs, arranged by Bob Caldwell, was on a railway paint crew. It was a hard job; we worked from daylight to dark and painted everything the foreman told us to, even if it made no sense. One day in the dead of the winter, our paint gang was somewhere near Bristol when the boss left for another assignment with the instructions, "You boys paint the damned water tower." So paint it we did, including the ice covering the outside of the tank. It was a fine moment, still vivid in my memory in the strange and wonderful way that the past hangs around.

Sacred too in my memory, even after all these years have passed, is the vision of my Rose Ellen standing at the Depot as we awaited the local train to take us to Radford to buy groceries for the week. Rosie was holding our newborn boy while I had a sack of fried baloney and mustard sandwiches, accompanied by two of the small bottles of Coke—all meant to tide us over until we got back to Belspring. For $5 we bought groceries enough to last seven days. It was all I could carry, since Rosie could only hold the baby. Those days of young adulthood were as pleasant as any I have ever known—and the Depot and trains have helped shape my notion of what Heaven may be like.

CHAPTER 10

Two Old Men:
John Harkrader & Bill Bruce

The Belspring I remember best was shaped by the characters who lived there. For me, these folks were the salt of the earth that gave laughter and the bittersweet taste of the fullness of life. Many of their stories follow.

OLD MAN JOHN HARKRADER (Hark to most of us) lived directly across the street from the Caldwells when I first came to live in Belspring in 1926. By any standard he was a character who fortunately lived close at hand. Of course, like all of us who lived in Belspring in those days, his worldview was a fairly narrow one, but it was funny and down-to-earth. Hark's understanding of life came in large part from the Bible, especially the way the Russellites interpreted it. As I came to know after I was grown, the Jehovah's Witnesses were hewn from the Russellite rock. They were called Russellites after Charles Taze Russell, who started the movement; they were characterized by a desire to recapture religion as it was in biblical times. As a good Russellite, Hark looked for the imminent Second Coming of Jesus and he harped a lot about hellfire. In my judgment, he talked crazy about religion and thus joined a noble group of folks in Belspring and down through the whole history of religion. At least that's the way it seems to me.

Whether in line with—or contrary to—the Russellites, Hark liked the New Testament passage about Jesus turning water to wine and Paul's advice to Timothy to "have a little wine for his stomach's sake." So, with that authority, he took the Concord grapes from his Belspring vines and fermented homemade fruit of the vine. Officially, Belspring was a hotbed for Christian temperance, but in fact most of the male population thought alcoholic beverages were Heaven's own elixir. One Lord's Day afternoon, siphoning his wine from wooden barrels into glass jars, Old Man Hark sampled a tad too much. He thought it was good, very good in fact, so he siphoned and sampled some more. By the time he quit siphoning he was as drunk as Noah after he dry-landed the ark on Mt. Ararat (Genesis 9). Hark passed out in his own basement and fell head first into one of the barrels and "damned near drownded," said Mr. Frazier, a good Methodist steward from across the road.

Adding to Old Man Hark's religious reputation, he took off warts and drove the fire out of a burn. Whether this was a biblical sign or not was subject to much store discussion on Calhoun's front porch benches. When I was a boy of ten, I went to Old Man with warts all over my hands. He rubbed his hands over them and said: "Boy, I can't take warts off. You go home now and don't talk foolishness." So, I did and forgot about it and in a few days the warts were gone. Hark's renown as a wart healer spread among the Methodists and Baptists, even to the Presbyterians, who had little use for miracles or Russellites, but liked getting rid of warts.

On another day discussing religious matters, Hark and John Hypes got in an argument on the porch of Calhoun's Store, presumably about one of the religious tracts of Taze Russell, which Hark had distributed to one and all on the porch. To settle the debate, Hark took a pick handle out of the store's bin and knocked out Hypes colder than a wedge. Hark's version of truth and righteousness had prevailed for one day. When he was asked about the knockout, he replied: "Sound my time, sir; I just tapped him with a weed, and he passed out."

Lest you think Hypes was a flower child, a few months later, Hypes shot and killed a Ledford fellow at Harold McCoy's Store in Parrott. The trial was held in the front room of Uncle Dick Bruce's house on Depot Street in Belspring. Being Uncle Dick's nephew, I watched the proceedings from the yard outside the house; Hark, of course, was present to check out the trial as well. It was summertime and the windows were raised and it was the best show in town. Anyone who wanted to could come and watch the wheels of justice turning. When the verdict came in, Hypes was sent to the state pen and died there.

Hark, a firm believer in old-time religion and old-time ways, had a difficult time accepting new inventions of the day including the first radio heard in Belspring. It was an Atwater-Kent in a big, unwieldy wooden box. Ted Wood, who was dating the Caldwells' daughter, Bertha, brought it down from Pennsylvania and hooked it to a car battery—no electricity in Belspring then. Crackling voices came from the speakers causing great consternation from Old Man Hark. When Wood explained that the sounds were radio signals, Hark was clear: "No sir, no sech thing as radio signals; them's spirits in the air." This kind of thinking was in the Belspring air; my dad's wife number three, Ethel, kept up the spirit of Hark's radio-wave skepticism—when the TV pictures of Neil Armstrong on the moon came over the airwaves, she would have no part of it: "No man has step't foot on the moon; they's set that up in a studio." Come to think of it, Ethel could also take off warts and take out fire.

When Old Man Harkrader died, the world was not as interesting a place as it had been. But Hark has lived on, in stories that still give pleasure.

I must confess that my cousin, William Amos Bruce (Old Man Bill to me), from Bland County, was also a latter-day Russellite. Bill, the namesake of my great-granddaddy Bruce, freely distributed *The Watchtower*, the official magazine of the Russellites and the Jehovah's Witnesses, out of the back of his panel van. Once he even went up to Washington DC with the intent to evangelize the folks of the nation's capital to his way of believing. He walked the streets for a few days, distributing *The Watchtower*, and when he returned he came to see me and reported, "You know, Bobby, the whole time I was there I never see'd one soul I knowed." Of course, he was from Bland County and knew lots of folks there, but Washington DC was not Bland County where there were not even five thousand people in the whole county.

I thank God for Old Man Hark and Old Man Bill. In their own ways, they were wonderful people and made life a sight to see and a tale to tell.

"Drink no longer water but use a little wine for thy stomach's sake and thine often infirmities."

I Timothy 5:23. KJV

CHAPTER 11

Etta Long, A Force of Nature

When Old Man Hark had passed from the scene, his home was bought by a worthy successor, Etta Long, her husband Frank, and their son Curtie. Who could have imagined that anyone could be as big a character as Hark, but in her way, Etta was every bit his match if not more. She stood no more than four feet, five inches and was about as broad as tall — but she was a force of nature.

ETTA LINKOUS LONG EPITOMIZED THE HOSPITALITY and orneriness of Belspring all wrapped together in a fire hydrant-shaped body. As everyone in our little village knew, the whole Linkous family were characters, but none of them quite matched Etta. Etta carried her strong personality and insistent ways into her married life with Frank Long, who likely got far more than he bargained for in his marriage. Etta was a formidable wife and mother to Curtie, a great friend, and a take-no-prisoners foe. She made Belspring life much more interesting than ever it could have been without her. Old Man Hark would have been proud.

Her personality certainly enriched the Belspring Methodist Church. All the Linkouses were big Methodists at the church and were ever eager in the church or community to sing as a family group: Etta, Charlie, Emmett, Mae Linkous Caldwell, and maybe one or two others whose names escape me. They thought themselves pretty talented, worthy of the radio. However, in fact, they were usually off-key and somewhat painful to hear, but sing they did, at every possible opportunity. Etta, as everyone who knew her recalls, brooked no criticism of her family. To her, critics simply didn't appreciate a good thing when they heard it. Their opinions rolled like water off a duck's back. To Etta, her folks could sing!

Etta stayed fiercely loyal to the Methodists until the big perfect-attendance-pin controversy began. As is not uncommon, the church had a hard time making financial ends meet, so a new preacher proposed to the board that the pins, which were outward symbols of piety and faith, only be purchased and given for the first two or three years of perfect attendance. A big brouhaha ensued, which kept the Methodists and the other churches fired up and entertained for weeks as this was in the days before TV and not much radio. In part, Etta lived for a good fight and she was ready for anything that affected her family. After all, between herself and Curtie, they each had accumulated many years of perfect attendance pins— enough to run from the shoulder of her dress to the floor. Those pins represented their badge of honor to God, and Etta intended to add many more. Husband Frank didn't go to Sunday School and had no interest in pins, except he certainly would not cross Etta.

The heat was on in the community and the Methodist board caught it from all directions, so they proposed a compromise: The church would order and pay for the first three years—after that they would still order, but folks had to pay for their own pins. Seemed reasonable, but Etta turned on the pressure, lobbying not only the Methodists, but also the Baptists and even the Presbyterians. She was playing to win, even if she had to oppose the preacher. After all, she was going to be around much longer than the preacher.

When the big vote came, emotions were high. Arthur Frazier, a steward in the church and neighbor of both the Caldwells and the Longs, made the motion to approve the compromise. It passed. Bob Caldwell, ever the hothead, threatened his neighbor, Arthur, with a pig-sticker that Bob just happened to bring with him to the meeting. Yes, it happened right there in the old Methodist church across from the Browns' property. I guess he knew if he didn't do something, his sister-in-law Etta would not let him hear the end of it. But that's the way the vote stayed. The compromise was approved. Eventually Etta and the rest of the Linkous crowd left the Belspring Methodist Church but came back after some time passed even though it was apparent she had lost—besides, she missed all those old friends. When she came back, most folks were glad for the renewal of Christian ties; they had missed Miss Etta.

The woods are full of Etta stories, but only two more will be mentioned in this narrative. One is of something as mundane as her potato salad. Everyone raved about it, including me. When Rosie and I married in 1939, we at first lived with Aunt Fanny, across the road from the Longs. Etta invited the newlyweds to supper, served us country ham and her famous potato salad. I dug in to a salad that had stayed a mite too long in the sun and I came down with a case of food poisoning, which had me at one point wishing for death. I recovered, never again to eat one bite of anyone's potato salad and I will go to my deathbed without another taste.

The last story is about Etta and her casket—it's all true, but it seems like it's made up. Etta was ever present for all funerals with a Belspring/Parrott connection. For love or money, she never missed a Belspring or Parrott occasion of death, even if at times it required a drive to Fairlawn or Radford. She was particularly a fan of the wakes and funerals of Perfater's Funeral Home (and later DeVilbiss, who took over for Perfater). In the wintertime, with her dark heavy coat and many years of perfect attendance pins, she brought to mind a short Russian field marshal surveying the troops. Dan DeVilbiss and his funeral gang of workers loved to see her coming, for they knew that particular wake or funeral would be worth the price of admission.

As Etta aged, she became concerned about the look of her casket at the funeral home and up front at Belspring Methodist—she was long since back in Methodist graces. And she did want to make a good exit! So, years before she died, she selected and paid for her casket. When she came down to final selection day, she went to DeVilbiss' funeral home in Radford and told Dan she had made up her mind, but before she made it final and paid her money, she wanted to try it out and see if the comfort level suited her. Dan and his right-hand man, Johnny Hubble, fetched a step stool and helped Miss Etta into her eventual final bed. She lay down, closed her eyes for a stretch, declared it suitable for a long sleep, and climbed out. Dan said he had been in the business a long time and that was the one and only time such a thing occurred.

Etta Linkous Long. She was a Belspring original. May her spirit, now free from death, sing on, sing on!

"And when from death I'm free, I'll sing on, I'll sing on. And when from death I'm free, I'll sing on. And when from death I'm free, I'll sing and joyful be and through eternity, I'll sing on, I'll sing on."

"What Wondrous Love is This?"
American folk hymn
First in written form in 1811,
Lynchburg, Virginia camp meeting

CHAPTER 12

Bob Caldwell's Life as Church Deacon, Boozer & Shotgun Wielder

My neighbor friend in boyhood, Methodist deacon, scoundrel, boozehound, chief "amen" guy from his Sunday morning pew in church, Doley and Fanny's son.

BOB CALDWELL'S STORIES COULD FILL A BOOK, and this larger-than-life Belspring character certainly impacted the boy I was and the man I became, so a few "Bob Caldwell" stories are necessary for this narrative. Bob was one of the solid members of Belspring's good-ol'-boys club, which meant he was a solid mixture of good and bad. He moved easily between Friday night bouts of heavy drinking and Sunday morning "amens" from his favorite Methodist pew. He was no different than the run-of-the-mill Belspring guy, which included most of us.

When I was no more than ten or twelve, there occurred a Bob Caldwell incident that I have laughed about for years. On a bright, cold February winter's day, I headed uptown from the Depot station. It was bitterly cold. In the frozen ditch off Depot Street sat none other than Robert "Bob" Caldwell, thirty-year-old son of Doley and Fanny. He had his trusty 410-gauge shotgun with him, with every intention, so he told me, of "killing that sumbitch who was trying to spark with Mae" (Bob's wife). The sumbitch was Frank, who worked for the Norfolk & Western as a trackwalker and may have sidelined as a romancer of Belspring's bored housewives.

Alley rumor hinted that Mae would hang her drying laundry upside down on the clothesline if Bob was gone and the coast was clear for Frank to visit. If the rumor was true, the situation was part of the agony and ecstasy of life: out of time and season, Cupid's arrow had struck Mae and Frank. On the alley circuit, no secret or code was safe from the ever-present need to enliven life by sharing some forbidden information; the upside-down-clothes code was broken. Word soon came to Bob. Thus, his ditch-side trap was ready to spring.

Just so, the Bob and Mae story, whether true or not, was unbelievably rich gossip. Of course, gossip was the coin of the alley realm and word soon came to everyone, including Bob. Thus, his ditch-side trap was set and ready to spring. No doubt in Bob's mind and imagination it was to be a swift and just killing. Messing with someone's woman was serious business and no jury in Pulaski County in those days would have given him more than a week in jail.

That particular February day, I was instructed by Bob to ignore his presence in the ditch—and his intentions too—and above all, I was to keep my mouth shut, which I did until long after Bob rested with his ancestors. As the day unfolded, Bob did not shoot anyone from his ditch-stand. Either the clothesline network had warned Frank away, or he never intended to come up Depot Street, or Bob had an overactive imagination, or, as the folks in Belspring tended to believe, it wasn't Frank's day to meet his maker.

Good thing too, for in the judgment of the clothesline-hanging ladies along the back alley, Frank's report card for life up to that point was likely to earn him a one-way ticket to Hell. If his time had come in 1929, his train was not bound for glory; it was headed in the wrong direction.

Though Bob and Mae and Frank are long dead, and I am not long for life myself, this story has lived on in my imagination. I tell it now because I like to think that there is not only humor and pathos in this tale, but also a truth as old as the human family: we live, we love, we find passion and meaning and laughter in surprising places, and we cling to these matters as the very stuff of our lives.

Another Bob story. Since I grew up in the Fanny and Doley Caldwell house and Bob and his wife, Mae, lived right behind us, Bob was like an older brother and mentor to me. As I grew into my later teenage years, Bob tutored me in some of the finer points of life, illustrated by what happened on a summer Saturday when Aunt Fanny asked Bob and me to dig a new Johnny-hole. We started early to take advantage of the cool morning and dug a fine new hole and used the dirt to fill in the old hole.

Before we moved the outhouse onto the new hole, Bob suggested that some refreshment from Shine Bland, the moonshine man, was in order. With lively step we were up the alley to Shine's Garage for a quart of his whiskey. It went down smooth and definitely helped our effort in moving the outhouse onto the new hole. When Aunt Fanny came out to inspect, she pointed out the fact that it was crooked on the hole, so it was back to moving the o-house. With Fanny safely back in the house we had a little more of Shine's finest and then rested in the shade waiting for the proper moving moment.

After refreshment, we again moved the house onto the new hole. Mother Nature intervened—it rained hard—so our second try also missed the hole. By the time we got that john on the hole in proper order we were covered in red mud but were convinced it was one of our finest moments. Triumphant, with the Johnny and hole properly aligned, we high-fived one another and headed into the house with our glad news; Fanny, of course, would not let us in until we hosed off and stripped down. All in all, a very satisfactory Saturday.

CHAPTER 13

Old Man Bush Wood
& Howard (Jiggs) Bruce

In my boyhood days everyone liked Bush Wood, the postman.
He was contact with the outside world through mail delivery; he liked his
job and treated folks with respect and kindness. Bush could have been
mayor if they had needed such an office. My first cousin, Jiggs Bruce,
was on the opposite side of the likeable scale: not well-liked,
but well-feared — at least by boys and young men.

IN BYGONE DAYS, as I have said at other places, I
called many an older man *old man*. Such was true for Bush
Wood. He was Old Man Bush for me and the people of
Belspring, although he was probably no more than fifty
years old. Old Man Bush was the mailman, and as such,
he was like a public official in a town that had none of
those, except Uncle Dick Bruce, Justice of the Peace, who
carried no gun or badge, and unofficial Game Warden
Malley Whitlock, who doubled as a town drunk and
comedian.

In the 1920s and '30s, the Rural Free Delivery (RFD)
service of Belspring and surrounding area depended on
Bush, who guided his trusty Model T through rain, sleet,
snow, biting dogs, and rising creeks to deliver the mail.
Bush was punctual, except for the times when his Model
T ran through a fence or gate and slowed the mail; he was

well known as a terrible driver. Old Man boarded at the home of the Zant Morans on Depot Street extension— just beyond Calhoun's Store. Zant and his peg-leg wife had two children, John and Gracie; Gracie was an epileptic. Bush liked the family and the children, and his bit of rent was helpful to them. He was like their uncle. He was a good, gentle, long-suffering man, who was lucky there was no such thing as a driving test in those days, and also lucky that the T did not go over thirty miles per hour.

The slow engine protected the citizens and dogs of Belspring and environs and Moran's garage protected Bush's T. The garage also offered opportunity for pranks on this good-natured guy who had one of the few cars in town. I remember the time a gang of us boys waited in the tall grass for him to park in the garage. Once he pulled in, we threw the doors shut and locked him in place with a two-by-four; there he was, trapped with his Model T in the garage. He spent some anxious moments before a family member heard him and freed the postal service from captivity. That incident was only one of several dirty tricks played on Bush.

On good weather days, Bush walked to the post office at Buckland's Store, then walked down Depot Street to the station with the mailbag in hand for the evening train. At the Depot, he picked up the mail that came in on the morning train and walked up the Kirkwood road and pasture back to the post office. His route was well known and unvarying. One summer day, Malcolm Hess, slightly older than me, dealt with his out-of-school boredom by hatching a special surprise for Bush, a surprise that waited at the wooden walking bridge across the branch that ran through Kirkwood land. Along came Bush with the mail and his unwavering trust in the human family; he stepped on the board, which was sawed from the bottom by Malcolm, and down came Old Man with his dignity and the mail into the branch. Malcolm spread the story wide, even as far as Parrott and Dry Branch. Bush, unhurt, took it in stride and went about his business.

In a couple of years Malcolm finished school in Belspring and went to work at the Lynchburg Foundry in Radford, the Radford Pipe Shop we called it. His first week at work, a crane accidently dumped metal on him and he died on the spot. The people of Belspring, including Bush, grieved for this son of the community, who now these eighty or ninety years later, is partly remembered for dumping Old Man Bush into the creek branch. A Belspring version of immortality, I suppose.

Bush was a good and patient man, liked by all, but one summer week he almost lost it. It started innocently enough: While Bush was in Buckland's Store sorting the mail, Jiggs Bruce, Uncle Dick's oldest boy and my first cousin, got a couple of other boys to help lift the back of the Model T and place pop crates under the rear axle so that the back wheels were barely off the ground. Bush came out, ready to do his rounds, cranked the T, hopped in, put her in gear...and nothing happened. He got out, looked around the car, saw nothing out of the ordinary and tried again. Meanwhile, the men and boys on the porch rolled in laughter. Eventually he discovered his problem and a couple of friendly sorts helped him on his way.

It may have been that same week when a final straw broke his calm demeanor. Enough was enough! It happened this way: Bush pulled out of the Morans' garage on his way to the post office but stopped at Calhoun's Store for a soda pop. When he came out, Jiggs Bruce was ready. Each time Bush cranked the Model T and fixed the spark then climbed in the car, Jiggs bolted off the porch, pulled the outside choke, and killed the engine. This happened about three times, then Bush calmly opened the car door, reached in the back, and pulled out his .22 rifle. He pointed the gun at Jiggs and told him if he choked out the car one more time he was going to be a dead Bruce, whether or not his daddy was justice of the peace.

It's not easy for a bully like Jiggs to back down, and I don't think Bush had any intention to shoot him, but Jiggs was uncertain enough that he never got up from the porch bench. The jig was up. Those on the store porch had, for a brief moment, thought they might witness the day Old Man Bush lost it and killed Jiggs Bruce, a shooting that would reverberate down the years. Killings happened from time to time in Parrott, but mostly from too much drink. A cold-blooded shooting on Calhoun's porch—that was more than one could fear or hope for. It proved what a good guy Old Man Bush was. Not many will remember him, but he was a good man.

Jiggs was a bigger and stronger boy than most and he was a bully. Regularly he came down to the Nesters, next door to me at the Caldwells', and dared any of the six boys to come out and fight him. No one took him up on the dare because he was tough. He was my first cousin and I liked him, but I always knew he was a bully, so I stayed on his good side. And I stood in awe of Jiggs. I was just a little runt of a boy, but he was big, and no one gave him any mouth. I still remember the sight and smell in Aunt Maggie Bruce's kitchen one hog-killing season when Jiggs made a sausage cake the size of a large cast-iron skillet, fried it up, and ate it along with a dozen biscuits. The sausage patty must have weighed two to three pounds. A big man with big appetites. When he was seventeen, he went to West Virginia to work in a coal mine; he got some young girl in a coal camp pregnant. He was set to marry her, but Uncle Dick, his daddy, went to the camp, gave the girl and her family some money, and brought Jiggs back to Belspring. When Jiggs finally married on the up and up, he and Kate had no children, and he never saw nor heard from his child in West Virginia.

One last Jiggs story. There was only one person I knew of who fought Jiggs to a standstill—that was Gump Morgan. Gump had lost his right hand or was born without it; he just had a stump. No one, including Jiggs, called him Gump the Stump to his face, because the end of his stump was bone and gristle. His punch was fearsome. One fight with Gump was enough for Jiggs. Even a bully has his limits before bone and gristle or a .22 rifle.

Jiggs turned out to be a very responsible adult. Had a good paying job at the Radford Pipe Shop, a salaried man, and was a well-respected Methodist lay preacher and a leading citizen in Radford, Virginia. He and Kate had a grand home near the doctors at old Radford Community Hospital. Never can tell how a boy will turn out, but Jiggs was a Belspring boy who made good when for a long time it looked like he would turn out bad.

"O Lord of life, where'er they be, safe in your own eternity, now live all your children gloriously. Alleluia! Alleluia! All souls you call, both here and there, do rest within your sheltering care; one providence alike they share. Alleluia! Alleluia!"
"O Lord of Life, Where'er They Be,"
Frederick Hosmer, 1888

CHAPTER 14

Lafayette Jackson &
Alfred Emmanuel Nester:
Just Call 'Em Fayt & Hickey

Our nearest neighbors on the Parrott side of Belspring were the Fayt Nesters: Mom and Dad with twelve children.

BELSPRING MORNINGS in the spring and summer of my childhood were gilded by Fayt Nester's deep bass voice, carrying over the pastures for what seemed like miles. Fayt tenant-farmed the land behind the Caldwell house. He and his team of horses swore their way across the landscape; actually, the horses were just an audience, Fayt was solo on the swearing.

"When morning gilds the skies, my heart awaking cries..."
"When Morning Gilds the Skies,"
German hymn translated by Edward Caswall, 1854

Except when he was working his horses, I don't remember Fayt swearing. But cuss he could when he was plowing and his swear words were better than the proverbial sailor. If the Belspring sky had not already been blue, he would have turned it so—words like a blue streak skipping over the farmland. I suppose the swearing was music to the horses' ears, for they responded with enthusiasm. I asked him once why he did it and his response was simply: "Horses love it." I nodded, for I sure did love it, too. It was a delight to a boy who never heard anything stronger than Uncle Doley's: "What in tarnation are you doing, boy?"

A goodly number of Belspring and Parrott men could cuss up a storm, but Mr. Fayt at work with his horses, well, he won the blue ribbon. At home Mrs. Nester didn't allow it, but in the pasture, he was free to practice his art.

Fayt and wife had twelve children: six boys and six girls. So many children that they hardly noticed the small Bruce boy with a big appetite who sat down to eat with them on many an occasion. Since I was the only child at the Caldwells' table, it was a nice change of pace to sit at a table surrounded by fourteen to twenty people, in-laws included. The supper table was filled with laughter and the delicious ever-present possibility of conflict.

The Nesters I knew best were Mr. Fayt and one of the sons, Hickey, who was about my age. As a boy, Hickey was a mess, hard to tell what he might do, and he continued on that path as long as I knew him. He avoided any farm work when he could because he saw how hard Fayt worked, so rather than farming chores, Hickey did one thing and then another, avoiding any steady work. I guess the one constant throughout his life was that he wasn't constant about anything, except following in his daddy's footsteps, he was a good cusser.

Still a teenager, Hickey went with my dad and brother Clyde to work on the Conowingo Dam on the Susquehanna River along the Maryland/Pennsylvania border. The project needed common laborers, and Hickey was about as common as workers came. At the dam site he roomed with Dad and Clyde. Clyde saved his quarters and half dollars for something special—only he knew the hiding place, or so he thought. One morning, Hickey up and quit his job and by the time Dad and Clyde got in from work, Hickey had cleared out, and cleaned out too. No more cache of coins. Later on, Clyde told me and Dad, "I know that low-down Hickey took them and if I can ever prove it, I am going to beat the living shit out of him." No proof ever appeared.

Safe back in the bosom of Belspring, Hickey and one of his buddies hired out to a guy building a house on Highland Road—their claim was to be experienced framers. Truth was, they didn't know shit from shinola about framing, but exaggeration they knew well. They framed the house quickly so as to get the job over with. Then, well satisfied, they left for the day. During the night a storm blew in; the framing collapsed in a hapless pile and a promising carpentry career was nipped in the bud.

Jobless again, Hickey took up the challenge offered by a promoter out of Pulaski. One hundred dollars could be won by any Pulaski County resident who lasted three rounds with a professional boxer. Hickey bought boxing shorts and ran the streets of Belspring and Parrott jabbing the air, telling one and all what he was about to do. The night of his debut, he and his entourage descended on Pulaski with much anticipation of what they would do with $100. The bell rang to begin round one and Hickey danced and feinted around the ring, then closed on the pro that stood watching. One punch square on Hickey's chin, and Hickey was blessed with a new nickname.

Belspring ridicule awaited *Old Glass Jaw* at the post office and on every storefront porch the following morning. Next thing we knew, Hickey left town and moved to West Virginia. Eventually he married, but domestic violence ended with a prison term for accidently killing his wife (with a gun, no less). At some point in the 1940s he reappeared in Belspring dressed in an old Army uniform. His story was that he was wounded in France. The tale made the rounds and Mr. Arthur Brown of Belspring urged Hickey to join the Veterans of Foreign War's chapter in Radford. When he played hard to get, Mr. Brown asked me to work on Hickey and get him to join, since we were neighbors as boys. I had to level with Brown: "Mr. Brown, he ain't been in the Army. He bought that uniform in a surplus store. He's been in the pen in West Virginia for killing his wife." Thus, the end of Hickey's public acclaim.

But it's hard to keep a good man down and there were more jobs than men to take them at the Radford Arsenal, so eternal optimist that he was, Hickey was certain a high-paying job awaited. He hired on with the government and lasted one day, at least part of one day. Alcohol had to be used to make ammunition powder, but it was laced with benzene and was poison. Some of the men, much more clever about alcoholic drinks than anything else, discovered that if strained through a loaf of bread, the benzene was gone, and it made a plenty fine drink when mixed with pop or apple juice, or water if that's all you had. On lunch break Hickey sampled enough government whiskey that he was too drunk to work, so he was fired, and the guards had to carry him outside the gate and dump him on the ground. The government wanted no part of the Belspring boy.

But, wait, it is still hard to keep a good man down!

More jobs than men to take them. If the government didn't want him somebody else would, so Hickey hired on with a private contractor as a machinery mechanic. Asked to take apart a press used in making ammunition powder, clean it, and put it back together, he fell to it. He took it apart in record time, but putting it back together was another matter. Hickey persevered until the job was finished. One small problem—he had two or three parts left over. No problem: He took the extra parts to the dump and pitched them. Of course the press did not work, and someone found the discarded pieces in the dump and traced them back to Hickey. Once more, though this time sober, the guards escorted him back to the gate with the careful instructions that if he ever again showed his face at the Radford Army Ammunition Plant, he was to be arrested and jailed.

Soon thereafter Hickey disappeared for good from Belspring. I think now and then about my boyhood friend and the man he became. If nothing else, he gave those of us who knew him a treasure trove of good stories.

As for Mr. Fayt, he was a good man who provided for his family and took care of his horses. Anyone who heard Mr. Fayt with his horses will not forget those gilded mornings.

CHAPTER 15

San Fuquay,
Rastus Smith & the KKK

By the time of my arrival in Belspring, San Fuquay and Rastus, "Raz" Smith were the sole remnants of a once-thriving black community.

IN MANY WAYS, Belspring and Parrott were primarily railway villages. To accommodate the railway workers, shacks, proper houses and businesses sprang up around the tracks that ran down what is now Virginia Route 600. Some of the workers and their families stayed on and helped lay the new line down closer to the river and build the Depot. A goodly number of these Norfolk and Western construction workers were African American, of whom a few dozen owned land and houses in the Belspring section of Neck Creek. A black school and a couple of black churches were constructed, but by 1926 when I arrived, only two blacks remained in town: San Fuquay, who lived in his momma's old house on Neck Creek Road, and Rastus (Raz) Smith.

Raz was a tenant farmer and lived in a small house on the Brown farm down toward the New River. Later he became a house servant for the Browns. I did not know him well, though I followed him a few times as he plowed the Brown's cornfield with horses. Every once in a while, his plow turned up a Shawnee arrowhead from the tribe that once hunted in the fields along the river. Those discoveries spoke of a depth to life beyond anything I could yet imagine, though imagine I did about that other world.

Mostly I remember Raz from his chief Belspring claim to fame. Rastus was the child of ex-slaves and he said they had taught him to trumpet like an African elephant. Who knows the actual story—maybe he had been to a circus in Radford and heard one of the show elephants, but Raz claimed it came natural to him; it was in his people's blood. Years later, I finally came to the conclusion that it was his joke on all the white folks. Whatever the actual story, with some frequency, he stood on the porch at Calhoun's Store and trumpeted like an elephant. It was a pretty impressive sound and Belspring folk appreciated it. So far as any of us knew, it was the only store front in those parts on which, if you were lucky, you might hear the sound of a genuine African elephant trumpeting come down Depot Street. All that sound from this lone child of slaves.

"In my trials, Lord, walk with me. In my trials, Lord, walk with me; when my heart is almost breaking, Lord, I want Jesus to walk with me."

Negro spiritual

The other black person in town was San. Wounded in a knife fight when he was young, he had only partial use of one arm and leg and a big ugly scar on his neck. He walked with the aid of homemade crutches. In addition to being coal-black in a white village, his knife scars made him the subject of much interest and speculation and a little fear. San never worked that I knew of, but I did know firsthand—as did all baseball-loving folk—that he was a big baseball fan. At every ball game on the Belspring School field, San had his usual spot behind the backstop at home plate—he helped the ump call balls and strikes, unofficial but definite. He was tolerated and occasionally cheered by the fans because he saw things in favor of the home team. He was practically the definition of a *homer ump*.

San's house in the black end of Neck Creek Road was next to that of Malley Whitlock and his son, Ortie. More or less my age, Ortie had an unending curiosity about anything happening at the Fuquays'. From childhood he knew of the widely spaced boards in the Fuquay floor that gave someone who crawled under the house a slitted-view of the household. When San's son married and brought his bride to Belspring, Ortie's under-the-floor knowledge came in handy. According to Ortie, known to be an irascible truth-teller and sometimes a liar, San fancied the son's young bride. According to Ortie, San and his son chased that poor girl all over the house. Honeymoon over, they departed, except the imaginations in the Whitlock household were whetted for months to come.

Both San and Raz had to endure the rampant racism that was true of Belspring and Parrott. From 1926 to 1940, when I knew Belspring/Parrott on a daily basis, racism was bad. Two black families lived in that small white community that had its own chapter of the KKK. Hard to believe, but it's true. When I was a boy, I watched Bob Caldwell as he came to Doley and Fanny's house and put on his robe and hood, then walked over to Calhoun's Store where the noble knights met in a big room on the second floor. That's where Rosie and I lived when our oldest son was born in 1941.

The Klan took a foothold among some men in Belspring/Parrott because of the scarcity of jobs brought on by the Depression. Folks needed someone to blame and the Klan said it was because of the blacks. So, although San and Raz were for the most part treated as a regular part of the community, they must have lived in fear of the white sheets. For sure, racism and hatred seem to know no bounds of sanity or decency, and most members of the KKK were cowards hidden under their robes. Even as a boy, I recognized that.

I know too that the racial prejudice and hatred by the Belspring/Parrott residents, although not as bad as it once was, still exists. It's shameful to say, but a black man does not want to be found in that end of the county when the sun goes down. Here and there Confederate flags still fly. I am glad that I have lived long enough to see Barack Obama as president of the United States; I am proud that America is that kind of country. Of course, Raz and San, long dead, could never in their wildest dreams imagine such a thing could happen.

CHAPTER 16

Hog-Killing Time and
The Death of Young Chester Whitlock

As in all Appalachian Mountain country, raising and butchering hogs was one of the most important community activities. Hog meat and lard were staples of life – a way to make it through the winter when living was hard.

THE WHITLOCKS' PLACE ON NECK CREEK ROAD was an unofficial hog butchering locale. Bright and early on killing day, usually a Saturday in November, Belspring folks went into their pigpen and shot their butchering hogs in the head and slit their throats. Rural folks know the literal meaning of "bleed like a stuck hog." Hog butchering was a yearly ritual and vital community event. Mountain people had been doing such since anyone remembered. At one time in the past, it meant survival, for in the cold of winter, hog meat and hog fat could see people through until gardens were planted. The 1930s were not that different from hardscrabble times in the past—no one had any money to speak of, so a hog butchered and put up was life itself. In some years after Rosie and I married, we butchered four hogs: two for us and two for Rosie's mother and dad.

Once the swine was killed, neighbors joined together to winch the hogs up a thick tree limb with a gambrel stick wedged between the tendons of both hind legs and let them bleed out good. As several generations knew, unless the hog was bled out, the meat would be red—no good for eating or preserving. Pink or white are the colors for pork.

Mid to late morning of killing day, a flatbed trailer hitched behind a horse combed the alleys and the hogs were tossed on the bed for the short ride to the Whitlocks'. Once arrived, they were dunked in the scalding drum filled with hot water to loosen the hair. Scraped, the head was wrenched from the carcass for removal of the brains for scrambling with eggs for breakfast. Snouts and other meat and the head went to make headcheese and souse. Fried souse and eggs made a good morning meal.

The neighborhood joined in the festive atmosphere. Men killed the hogs and did the major sawing and butchering. Women collected the lesser cuts intended for sausage and threw them into the barrel for later grinding. The delicacies—hams, chops, short ribs, roasts, loins— were set aside to be salted and seasoned and prepared for the smokehouse, which everyone had. Even the feet were used. Once they were sawed off, the process of pickled pig's feet began. A good pickled pig's foot is a delicacy for sure.

Most of the pig was used, but we didn't bother with the intestines for chitlins. I know they were highly treasured in black communities, but our black folks were mostly gone. Besides the smell was too high and strong; Rosie for one, wanted nothing to do with them. So, I've never eaten any chitlins, though folks who have say chitlins are good if you can stand the smell while they cook.

Of course, we cut up the fat back into useable portions for later use and lard was rendered from the snow drift section. It was all a regular pig orgy. Nothing quite like it in my experience, with overtones of a day when folks had to work together to survive. Those who experienced these days do not forget them. Now, of course, it's the tame, packaged meat section of Wal-Mart. Somehow the old way seemed more humane and human, but such a portrayal betrays my age. Ham, bacon, tenderloin, pork chops, and spare ribs—oh, makes an old man hungry to think about it. The smell of spare ribs and potatoes cooking may be my favorite food aroma.

"There is a fountain filled with blood...and sinners plunged beneath that flood lose all their guilty stains."

William Cowper, 1772

In my mind, the Whitlocks' place will forever be linked to that special time of the year and to Malley's boys, the Whitlock twins, Ortie and Chester. Like most twins, Ortie and Chester were best of friends and fierce rivals, almost like Jacob and Esau in the Bible. They liked to fight one another better than anyone else. For a five-cent pot, they would fight in the alley beside Buckland's Store. It was fierce; you thought they might kill one another. When one or the other finally called out "uncle," the fight was over, and they were again best of friends.

In the early years of World War II, Chester went into the Army. In basic training down in forsaken Louisiana, he raised his head too high in a field exercise and was shot in the head and killed. The Whitlocks mourned—and, as was often true in those awful years, the entire village grieved. We knew deep in our hearts that all was not right in the world or in us. All was especially not right for Ortie, for the other half of his self was gone. It was reported that Ortie, then an old man in the Radford hospital just before his death, lamented, "Chester, why did you raise your ugly head?"

Ortie never left Belspring. No Louisiana or flat land for him. He stayed where the rich memory of Chester and hog killing time lived on. He stayed where the creeks ran to the New River and where cow pasture baseball was a community event in which Ortie was a catcher of some renown. A left-handed batter, he was not much of a hitter. His other half, Chester, was the good hitter. All of us who ever saw those two boys fight over a nickel knew we had seen a struggle of almost biblical proportions. And to a man, a woman, or boy, we were deeply saddened by Chester's death and we hope to see him in Heaven someday. "When the trumpet of the Lord shall sound," we live in the hope that we will be there.

"When the trumpet of the Lord shall sound, and time shall be no more, and the morning breaks eternal bright and fair... I'll be there."

"When the Roll is Called Up Yonder,"
James Milton Black, 1893

CHAPTER 17

Jack & Boonie Carden

*The Cardens lived right across Belspring Road from the Caldwells.
They were as famous as it got for boys of the Road. Baseball, catfish,
polecats, coal mining, gospel music, and a shave and
haircut were their claims to fame.*

THE CARDEN BOYS WERE LEGENDS, older brother, Jack, the most so. He was a Belspring/Parrott hero. For one thing, lots of folks thought he would make it to the "show" (major league baseball). All those of us who saw him pitch on the cow pasture circuit knew we had seen greatness. Jack could fire a baseball like it was shot out of a cannon; no-hitters were the order of his pitching days. Before World War II, the Navy recruited him to the Brooklyn Shipyards to work a little and pitch a lot. He was good too. But when his hitch was up, he missed Belspring, Parrott, the mountains, and fishing on the New River too much. So homeward bound he was and never again left.

*"They cast their nets in Galilee, just off the hills of [Brown].
Such happy, simple fisher folk."*
"A Hymn of Peace," William Alexander Percy, 1924

It was a rare day when Jack wasn't on the river, at least for an hour or two. He was so good at catching fish that neighbors came to him and bought some of his catch—fresh out of the river. No store in Belspring or Parrott sold fresh fish, except for salt fish in a barrel that had to be soaked in water for a day before it was fried, but Jack sold his day's catch right out of his home and barber shop. Where else could you go for a G.I. haircut and also enough catfish to feed a family of fifteen?

In later years, Jack, a good Christian man, combined river fishing with fishing for the souls of men. Since it was generally assumed that women folk's souls had already been saved, evangelists concentrated on the menfolk. Jack's avocation was as a radio singer and soft-sell evangelist. It was the Radford station, WRAD, that carried his show. He mixed his Christian witness in with some truly awful mountain hymns; actually, the hymns were okay, but Jack and his guests were usually off-key. In truth, Jack could not sing a lick and his guests, like the Linkous family singers, were no improvement, but enough folks listened in and supported his program that it stayed on the air for years. My oldest boy said Jack should have stuck with fishing for fish rather than souls. But all in all, Jack was well known and well loved.

He was also a coal miner because the best money in those days came from working in the mines. In his later years, Jack gained some local fame for his mining days when Virginia Tech took an interest in the mines and the life of the miners in Parrott and they interviewed this well-known miner, barber, fisher, and soul-saver.

Like the fate of many a younger brother, Boonie Carden lived somewhat in Jack's shadow, except when it came to trapping and raising polecats. Boonie got into the skunk business to make money. Times were hard, and people did what they could to make ends meet. Everyone knew that a pelt buyer came through twice a year and an unblemished skunk pelt was highly prized. So Boonie trapped polecats, as we called them, and sold a few pelts and made some money. Naturally his mind turned to larger profits, so he built some cages, trapped some black and white skunks and hoped they were horny enough to produce little polecats.

The polecat farm was in the side of the high bank along Route 600 in front of the Cardens' house and right across the road from where I grew up at the Caldwells'. At one time, as late as 1900, Route 600 ran along the N&W main line before it moved down nearer the river, so the road bank was high—ideal for Boonie's purposes. He dug into the road bed, imbedded wire cages, and waited for the cash to flow in. In another time and place, he might have become an entrepreneur with the Route 600 Polecat Farm as the beginning of his days as a rich man.

The dream was good, and all was fine, except for the occasional acrid odor arising along the road, but folks were used to skunk smell, so no one was too bothered by it. Unfortunately, a spring night ended that pastoral reverie in spectacular fashion. One of Belspring's hell-raisers, of which there were many, set the polecats free. The barking of dogs and a shout and curse here and there notified Boonie of their escape; his prized skunks were running all over Belspring. While folks were not unaccustomed to skunks or their perfume, this was an unusually large number and the odor saturated most of the town, the stink seeping through the floorboards of homes. Dogs were appreciative of the adventure, though a large number were sprayed, and folks used brooms to run the dogs out from their usual lairs under the houses.

Boonie recaptured a few; some made it into the woods and freedom; one or two were run over by an auto—even in those days before many cars were on the road. I suspect, though I don't remember, that some got shot with a kitchen shotgun. Women folks likely put pressure on husbands and sons to do something about the skunks running around.

It was the end of Boonie's business venture with skunks, but those alive in those days (if any of them are still alive and able to remember) will recall Boonie Carden and his skunks. It's part of our folklore.

"All creatures (skunks included) of our God and King, lift up your voice and with us sing: Alleluia!"

"All Creatures of Our God and King,"
Francis of Assisi, 1225
Material in parentheses added

CHAPTER 18

Hippy-Hoppy Nester, Malley Whitlock & Peter Green Hodge

Among the things that long life teaches is that each man and woman have their own dignity, their own special contribution to the human scene. While the behavior of some may not be my way, I take delight in the quirks and ways of people quite different from me, for they are certainly people who make life funnier and richer.

IT IS REMARKABLE the way the passing of years and the coming of age soften the sharp, hurtful—even mean-spirited—edge of people and things past. I've come to that place in life and I am grateful. Now, in my later years, I claim to know little about the judgment of God, except that it is gentle and kind, even toward the foolish and damaging things of life. From that perspective, I look upon some of the foolishness of people and matters long gone with affection and gratitude.

> *"Swift to its close ebbs out life's little day. Earth's joys grow dim, it's sorrows fade away."*
> "Abide with Me," Henry Francis Lyte, 1861

Certainly, I look upon Armstrong Nester, better known as Hippy-Hoppy, in that light. Hippy-Hoppy lived across the street from the Whitlocks and San Fuguay.

Hippy's nickname came from a strange little hop he had when he walked, particularly if he was angry. Hippy was what we today would call an alcoholic; he lived to take a drink and it was a constant source of trouble for him and his family.

Once, when I was a young adult, I was in Joe Newcombe's beer joint on the Fairlawn Road before it reached the Radford Bridge. Hippy had too much to drink and got in an argument with Joe Gordon, who lived at the back of the joint. The argument became heated, threats thickened the air and Joe hit Hippy in the head with a bat. Hippy was out like a light and when he awakened he barely remembered what they had been arguing about.

Hippy also frequently fought with his son-in-law, Wendell Ritter. Wendell, who was as mean as a striped rattlesnake, almost always got the best of it—he was younger and stronger. After one of their fights, Hippy came down the alley by the school and headed up the Neck Creek Road to his home; he was bleeding like a stuck hog and cussing Wendell at each step. It was warm weather and the schoolhouse windows were up; Hippy-Hoppy's swearing gave much joy to the hearts of all us boys in school that day.

As an aside on Hippy's son-in-law, Wendell, he and a fellow poker player (a guy by the last name of Wilson, as I remember) got into a heated dispute during a card game up on Back Creek. Wendell accused Wilson of cheating, pulled a pistol, and shot and killed him. The trial was one of many held at Uncle Dick Bruce's house on Depot Street and we sat outside on the grass and watched Wendell get thirty days in the Pulaski jail. The men of Belspring/Parrott took cheating at cards very seriously.

Yes, Hippy-Hoppy might be a drunk, but compared to Wendell he was as pure as the driven snow.

Malley Whitlock and Peter Green Hodge were likewise characters of some renown. Malley and his twin sons, Ortie and Chester, were the neighbors of the Fuguays and Hippy-Hoppy. Somehow Malley finagled an appointment as unofficial game warden of Belspring and Parrott. With this new lease on life, he sent off and received by mail order a generic uniform to confirm his appointment. Of course, Malley proceeded to parade around town as if he were an elected official who could dispense justice as he saw fit. He was popular, too, with the way he conducted his game warden job—Malley never fined anyone who lived in Belspring or Parrott for hunting or fishing irregularities. However, if someone was from any other town or county, God help them because he milked them for every offense he could. In a sense, it was really a con for out-of-towners.

The sheriff's department and Uncle Dick Bruce, Justice of the Peace, sometimes used Malley to serve a warrant, which was the occasion when Malley served Peter Green Hodge up on Parrott Mountain. Peter was a notorious liar, drunk, and ne'er-do-well, even by Parrott standards, so up the mountain went Malley in his official-looking uniform. He found Peter Green drunk as a coot, firing a gun into the air. Of course, Peter and Malley knew each other, and Peter offered Malley a friendly drink of moonshine. It so happened Malley liked whiskey much better than he liked serving warrants, so the two of them had several friendly drinks and soon there were two drunks rather than one, both firing guns in the air, shouting and swearing and making the awfulest racket.

Before long, someone reported the gunshots to Uncle Dick, who called the law to come from Pulaski. Up the mountain went the reluctant deputy, found the two drunks, and arrested both. Down the mountain road they came headed to Belspring and Pulaski. When they drove by Buckland's Store and post office, a big crowd of men, boys, and women too had heard of the commotion and gathered to see whatever they could. The deputy drove slowly by the store, so the assembled crowd could glimpse the excitement. There, Peter and Malley (still in his uniform) were in the back seat of the car with Malley waving to those gathered on Buckland's porch as if he were the key figure in a patriotic parade. A couple of days later, Malley in his dirty and crumbled uniform returned to his unofficial duty as game warden. Peter Green was back home as well—remorseful, but glad for the attention.

Thus, at home, Peter was primed to once again get saved at a local revival. Revival preachers were right fond of Peter; he gave them a good target and if he showed up for the revival, he was seventy-five percent certain to be saved again! The saving never took for long, though—he liked drinking and carousing too much to be sober and saved all the time. Some folks liked to believe Peter might one day get saved and it would take, but they were fooling themselves, for as the saying goes, "he can't any more change than a chicken weasel can quit sucking blood."

I was a young boy when Malley and Peter shot up the air on Parrott Mountain. By that time, I had lived in Belspring long enough to believe it was the best possible place for a boy to live. Of course, I heard the stories of Malley and Peter over and over as I was growing up. It always got better with each telling.

"Shall we gather at the river? Yes, we'll gather at the river, the beautiful, the beautiful river. Gather with the saints at the river that flows by the throne of God."

"Shall We Gather at the River?" Robert Lowry, 1864

CHAPTER 19

Shine Bland & Other Bootleggers
and Drinkers of Renown

*Belspring and Parrott were at one time hard-drinking places. Men spent
much of the time finding or making alcoholic drinks. Bootleggers who
ensured a ready supply were as respected as preachers,
though on the opposite end of the pole.*

I'VE BEEN A TEETOTALER since I was thirty
years old, except for the time I had a stein of beer with
my two sons and one of my grandsons in Munich,
Germany. They wanted me to hoist one as a celebration
of our trip, so I did, but the imbibing of whiskey or beer
or wine has not been a part of my life for sixty years. I'm
glad I quit when I was young, for no good ever came of
taking a slug of whiskey, but until the time I decided that,
I was a full-fledged member of the Belspring tradition
where nearly all men (except maybe preachers) took a
drink. And since this is a tale of my youthful years, it's
natural for me to talk about what we did, and the ones
who enabled us to drink whiskey were an important part
of that story.

Of course, in my youth there only two
viewpoints on drinking: either you did it, which meant
you were a sinner and likely drunkard, or you did not
drink and were among the righteous Christians of life.

There was no middle ground. It was a religious issue of the highest order. But this is a story of drinkers and those who gave them what they wanted.

One was Shine Bland, the Moonshine Man. Talk about a nickname that fit the man—Shine had it! I'm not sure when he went into the bootleg business, but he was hard at it when I moved to Belspring in 1926. Of course, he sold only moonshine in those early years, for no legal distilling happened during Prohibition. I'm not certain where his shine came from, but stills were always running on the creeks of Belspring and up on the back roads of Parrott Mountain in those days. Folks wanted a drink; money was to be made and corn turned to whiskey was a lot more profitable than feeding it to cows or pigs.

Shine ran a garage near the Belspring Baptist Church and he fixed cars now and then, but his chief moneymaking job was selling whiskey out of the garage. For a larger fee, he delivered it to the customers who didn't want to be seen at the garage. On Sunday mornings, Baptist men would pass Shine's Garage on the way to the nearby church, and though they may have been among his best customers, never a wave nor nod came his way. Folks, then more than now, liked to pretend that they were not doing something, when in fact, they almost lived for the next drink. Now, of course, we know alcoholism as a dread illness that ruined many a life, but in those days, whiskey was a treasured friend on the way to ignoring crying children, bossy wives, and the poverty that lingered near most everyone.

Truth was, Shine the Man was universally liked in Belspring/Parrott. He was the man who allowed us to scratch the itch we had for drink. He operated on a "cash only" basis, so he was not concerned about keeping records or trying to collect debts; if you had the money, you could buy the whiskey; bootleggers were no respecters of status. And Shine, like all good businessmen, was partial to regular customers, one of whom was Bob Caldwell, my friend, and Doley and Fanny's boy.

Safe from Mae Caldwell's sight, Shine delivered some whisky to Bob down at the Parrott Mine Commissary parking lot. Bob sat in his car and Shine delivered the goods through the window. When he heard the delivery fee, Bob argued with Shine and told him he had a mind to get out of the car and give Shine a black eye to match his name—threat delivered. It was a two-punch fight; Shine got in two punches before Bob got out the car. Two shiners all right, both belonging to Bob.

Robert Harkrader on Highland Road—no close kin to Old Man John Harkrader, the Russellite—was another well-known moonshiner. Robert married a Filipino lady, and this added to his local fame, for she was the only exotic person in those parts. In those days, people had deep prejudice against anyone of color: the deeper the color, the darker the prejudice. Robert's wife was light-skinned enough that she was only mildly resented as the outsider she was. Robert and the missus lived a good life, financed by his thriving whiskey business. They are both buried in the old Highland Methodist Church cemetery; his burial monument is one of the better ones, testimony to the male population's love for drink and Robert's vision of what people wanted.

Hensel "Bootlegger" McCoy from up on Back Creek was another man with the good name, but I don't think he ever sold much whiskey. He just drank it and was therefore well enough acquainted with the legitimate, real bootleggers to earn the moniker. There were other bootlegger wannabes—my dad, George, being one, but mostly Belspring was famous for drinkers more than sellers.

One of those best known to me was Dube Carden, a buddy of mine, who lived not far from the Caldwells. Dube loved to drink. His wife, as was true of all the Belspring women, was dead set against it. Dube's drinking frequently got him in a mess with her. One such instance happened on a trip to the Radford Community Hospital to visit his wife. Clyde and I drove him to the hospital, but on the way, he stopped for some moonshine for himself and flowers for his missus. By the time we arrived at the hospital room, a ward in those days, he'd had enough of the shine that he gave the flowers to the wrong woman. Thought she was pretty, I guess. The missus was not impressed.

And then there was the case of bad timing. Dube's wife left for a few days, rode the train to Bluefield to visit her sister. In her absence, he stocked up on beer and then, as luck would have it, she returned a couple of days earlier than planned. He saw her coming up the alley and frantically ran into the house, took the beer out of the icebox, and tossed it into the garden to rest among the squash and tomatoes, though the beer was his favorite crop.

The funniest incident I remember about Dube and his beer happened when the Methodist women were holding a Bible study in the Cardens' living room. To get out of the house, Dube and a buddy of his went to William's beer joint near the Radford Bridge over the New River. He downed a couple, then bought a poke full to take home. As he tiptoed by the women's meeting, headed for the icebox, the paper poke busted and sent beer bottles rolling through the women's prayer group. To hear Dube later recount the story was worth the price of admission;

the women's Bible study prayer meeting discussion dissolved into castigating drink in general, and Dube specifically. Both were somewhat worthy subjects.

All in all, Dube and Hensel and Bob were probably alcoholics before we ever knew to call them by that name. Shine and Robert drank very little, but were good capitalists, ready by hook or crook to make a buck. I enjoyed all those men and certainly in my own way admired them. The truth is they did about as well as was possible for them, given the time and circumstances of their lives.

"Oh, you can't get to Heaven on a bottle of gin, cause the Lord won't let no drunkards in. You'll never get to Heaven on a bottle of stout, cause the Lord he throws all drunkards out."

American folk tune

CHAPTER 20

The Sifford & Hamilton Feud

As we all know, there was a time in the mountains and hollers that clan or family feuds were not uncommon. Belspring/Parrott's version was between the Hamiltons and Siffords. What I always understood is that the feud centered around whiskey and debts.

AS FAR BACK AS THE CIVIL WAR, and likely a good many years before that, the Sifford clan had a still up on Back Creek. It stands to reason that it was one of the chief sources of their wealth—a wealth that allowed them to build and maintain the big Sifford house overlooking Back Creek, a house that still stands though it's long been out of Sifford hands.

The Hamilton clan was also prosperous, and for Parrott folks, they were once well off. Alexander Hamilton, born in the 1880s, inherited the bottom land on which the Belle-Hampton Coal Company was established. Unfortunately, Alexander also inherited the Hamilton tendency to drink too much. He was very bad to drink, and soon drank his prosperity dry on flights of fancy fueled by Sifford shine. To make matters worse, he failed to pay his debts to the Siffords. The love of drink and whiskey on credit was a deadly combination.

Alexander made plenty of money, but he drank it faster than he made it. Sad story, but true.

One of Alexander's sons, Otha, had the misfortune of being heir to the feud, and if he had lived long enough, perhaps the drinking too. The two-family battle continued and heightened until one late morning in the 1930s. Church was in session at the Parrott Church of God (now a United Methodist church). Otha Hamilton and two Sifford boys met at the entry of the church; hot words were exchanged and the Sifford boys gunned down Otha on the church steps. He died there before God and all the church people. My brother, Clyde, and his wife, Josephine, whose mother was a Hamilton, were in church that day.

One of the Sifford boys got twenty years in the state pen; the other drew ten years. The whole drama was a tragedy by any standard. No one still living has forgotten that sad, infamous deed.

The Hamiltons, who had such a bad history with whiskey, suffered an additional tragedy connected to the distilled elixir. Everett Hamilton and his son, Everett Junior, were on Parrott Mountain in a drink fest with Everett's brother, Charles. A disagreement provoked an argument, a fight ensued, and Charles was clocked in the head with a coal rock. He lived on for a month before he gave up the ghost. The story has echoes of Cain and Abel in Genesis, when Cain killed his brother. Thereafter Cain carried the mark of Abel's death, presumably the mark of guilt, for the rest of his life. Guilt like that was carried by Everett, Jr.

Alcohol played a major part in another Hamilton story. In 1950 or so, Pooh John Hamilton, back from a stint with the paratroopers, stood on the Back Creek bridge watching the flooded creek. He was fortified by whiskey, perhaps even from a Sifford still, so as a haystack floated along the flooded creek and went under the bridge, most of the stack was knocked off by the bridge, but when the remainder came out the other side, Pooh John jumped on for a ride. Perhaps someone had dared him, but paratrooper that he was, the jump was simple and the ride safe—until near the railway trestle where a whirlpool was created by the flood, the stack hit a tree limb and went under with Pooh John still aboard. Another Hamilton bites the dust, or in this case, the flood.

Those on the bridge were sure he was a goner, "drownded" as folks said it in those years, but after a stretch he came up the road wet as a rat, but spry as a cat with nine lives. I guess it gives credence to the saying: "God looks out for fools and drunks." Last I knew, Pooh John was still alive and well, living a sober and good life down along Back Creek. The Hamiltons are proud of their living legend.

CHAPTER 21

Getting Saved:
Revivals, Baptisms, & Such

*Every head bowed and every eye closed, as we sing one more verse of
"Just as I Am, without One Plea."*

EVEN NOW, SEVENTY-PLUS YEARS removed from those revival words, I hear, ever so faintly, the tinny gospel sound of a piano and smell the exotic mixture of sawdust and sweating bodies. Everyone who grew up in the Belspring/Parrott of nearly a hundred years ago knew these sounds and smells of salvation as surely as Catholics know the sound of clanging bells and the smell of incense.

In Protestant America in its revivalist form, we were taught in home, school, and church to believe that eternity was at stake in whether or not we went forward to the altar and made the decision for Jesus, or at the least rededicated ourselves to Him and his way. It was only these acts that could save us from the evils of drink, or sex outside marriage, or any kind of sensual sin, for without this dose of salvation we were bound for an everlasting fire. No matter the church—Baptist, Methodist, Presbyterian, Pentecostal—we knew this language and reality.

"Just as I am, Thou wilt receive, wilt welcome, pardon, cleanse, relieve. Because Thy promise I believe, O Lamb of God, I come, I come."

"Just as I Am," Charlotte Elliott, 1935

We didn't have any formal high churches like Catholics, Episcopalians, and the like. The only ones who came close were the Presbyterians who were considered as stiff and high-falutin' as Belspring churches got. But the Presbyterians were a far cry from high church—and besides, not many people swung to the predestined Presbyterian side of things.

I don't remember much of anything about church or religion before my life in Belspring. Dad wasn't a religious type, or at least not a church type. Mommie, on the other hand, was prone to be a fundamentalist who took the Bible literally. Not that I really remember this, but I heard stories told of her religious practices and piety. My older brother, Clyde, told of going with Mommie to a revival down the hill from Pearisburg in Liberty City. He was only eight or nine and I was too young to go. Clyde's version was full of frenzy and fear as people shouted and danced and swooned. Snakes were brought out of burlap bags and handled to prove faith in the Lord. Clyde was frightened enough to slip out of the tent and run through the dark up the steep hill to our house in Pearisburg.

Eventually, I was old enough to experience the Lord for myself. Of the revivals I remember, most were in the summertime when the living was hot and lazy; perhaps that helped the preaching and the plea for salvation, for we had less trouble trusting that Hell was hot, miserable and definitely not a place we wanted to be.

When I was about twelve, I went with some other boys to a Pentecostal revival up on Parrott Mountain. The preaching was loud and long, the prayers begged both God and congregation for the gift of the Spirit. Folks shouted, some danced in the Spirit; the aisles were filled. We stood outside the open windows under an apple tree, a gang of bored, disheveled mountain boys looking for something to do. Someone suggested we practice throwing apples. First one went through the open window and then another cut down on those filled with the Spirit. It was a mean thing to do, but we did it. Somehow the Lord chose not to strike us with a lightning bolt as we created chaos among the Pentecostal faithful.

Over the years I went to many a revival, and I would have to say that I did get spiritually revived at various times in my life, but I also did not give in easily to the revival hubbub. I suppose in some sense I was a resister because I liked to think through things. The most vivid example of this occurred at my home church, Belspring Methodist. I was a teenager and went to the revival service with my friend, Carroll McCoy. We went because there was nothing else more interesting to do in Belspring—it was long before the days of TV and most folks did not have a radio, so it was a revival to break the boredom.

The revival preacher of that night raised a moral storm about Heaven and Hell, righteous living and the dangers of being on the devil's side by drinking moonshine or running around with loose women. Following the sermon came the serious business of working the congregation up into an emotional frenzy to prepare them for being saved or for rededication. The hymns were geared toward this end:

"Almost persuaded now to believe..."
"There is a fountain filled with blood..."
"Revive us again, fill each heart with Thy love..."
"Softly and tenderly Jesus is calling..."

The biggest call of the night was for those who had never been saved at all to come forward and receive the gift of God's Spirit. I don't recall whether anyone did so that night, but if they did, much "praising of God" would have ensued. After the big call for salvation, it was time for rededication with the assumption that at the very least all wanted to do this, for this was the appeal to begin living anew for Jesus. In response, there were a number of people in the community who got saved several times over the years, but whatever happened on any given night, the evangelist had a plan and stuck to it. If folks did not come forward to the altar, he asked those in the pews to stand up if they had been saved. Finally, it was raise your hand if standing was too embarrassing.

That evangelical night in Belspring, all had come forward or stood or raised their hands except for two teenage boys: Bobby Bruce and Carroll McCoy. The evangelist took it as a personal challenge, so he came down to our pew and pleaded with us to get saved and be washed in the blood and forgiveness of Jesus and thus to avoid hellfire and damnation. The choir sang "Pass me not, O gentle Savior," so we stood up—not to be saved, but to escape. The evangelist followed us out the front door and down the church steps leading to Depot Street. We decided to make a run for it and up Depot Street we sprinted. Undeterred, the preacher ran after us, begging us to give ourselves over to Jesus. In the end we were younger and faster, so on that fateful night in about 1932, we were saved from being saved.

In time I did make a personal commitment to Jesus, but I did it in the privacy of my own mind and heart. It was between God and me, no preacher needed. Giving me personal space and leaving out manipulation and fear is one of the reasons that I have appreciated the Presbyterian church and I'm proud to say that most of my family has ended up Presbyterian.

Revivals and baptisms were, in their own way, wonderful events in the mountains. At times, they were the occasion for new beginnings, new hopes; at other times they were entertainment. One early spring, near Easter time, a revival came to Belspring and my old friend Ortie Whitlock got saved. His baptism was scheduled for the fishing hole on Back Creek, almost under the railroad trestle of the N&W, a common site of many a baptism over the years. On the Belspring side of the creek was a grassy slope, which was a pleasant place to picnic or watch a baptism. On Ortie's baptism day, family and friends and curious bystanders gathered on the bank and watched the preacher take Ortie out into mid-stream and put him under "in the name of the Father and Son and Holy Ghost." Ortie arose from the water a new man.

One of the bystanders that afternoon was Ortie's running mate, Brady Bane, fresh back from a prison stretch. Knowing that Back Creek was always cold, and particularly in the spring, Brady hollered out, "Is the creek cold, Ortie?"

"Nah" was the reply.

From the creek bank came Brady's rejoinder: "Better put him under again Preacher, 'cause he ain't quit lying."

Even with the humor and sometimes absurdity of church, I will say it has enriched my life beyond measure. For years, I taught Sunday School, washed dishes in soup kitchens, took meals to shut-ins, and visited the sick. I have been blessed by the opportunity to be of service to others and in that fashion to serve God. When all is said and done, I believe that is what faith and church are all about; the heart and soul of it is how you treat other people. I'm thankful the gentle Savior did not pass me by and that I have been privileged to live my life in His service.

CHAPTER 22

Random Tales of Local Lore

"And what more should I say? For time would fail me to tell of Gideon, Barak, Samson…and the prophets – who through faith conquered kingdoms…shut the mouths of lions…they wandered in deserts and mountains."

Hebrews 11:32-38

BUB TESTERMAN'S GARAGE is a piece of history carried only in the minds of old men like me, though once it was as alive as Sunday morning at the Methodist church. Lively and painted with oil and grease-stained overalls, old tires, and enough yarns to fill a young boy's mind plus a book or two. By the early 1930s, Belspring/Parrott had enough cars to warrant two garages: Bub Testerman's and Shine Bland's, but Shine's place was better known for whiskey, so he is not in this story. Bub's garage was on the main Belspring Road near the Depot Street corner and it was either a hangout for men who didn't want to go home to the wife or boys who needed to loiter—I was in the latter category.

Bub encouraged frittering an afternoon away. For a time, he had a hot dog stand, though I never had enough money to buy one. Bub's place also had a shock machine for entertainment. For one penny the machine sent an electric charge through handles; we discovered that if folks joined hands to shoulders, the shock was only received by the last one in line. For us it was a marvel; we loved the machine and the many shocks and laughs it gave us, especially when some unsuspecting soul stood at the end of the line.

Bub's was also the chief place for folks to get oil changed and tires gauged for long road trips, like driving the forty miles or so to the big railroad center of Roanoke. I was at the garage when an unnamed Parrott family got an oil change for a journey to see their daughter in the big city. They were excited to see their girl, who managed a Roanoke boarding house. Oil changed and tires gauged, they pulled out of Bub's for their adventure. Only after they were gone did Bub tell us that the so-called boarding house was actually one of many houses of ill repute that were in Roanoke's red-light district in those days. Like most funny stories, this one had a hint of the hard, even sad facts of life. In such small ways, Bub opened our minds to a broader world down Roanoke way—and God only knew what Richmond or Washington DC or New York might be like. In our hearts we knew, of course, that those far-off places could not possibly be filled with a more interesting life than the one that passed through Bub's doors and our lives.

In the manner of most folks from small hamlets, we might see other bigger places, but Belspring and Parrott already contained more life than we were able to fully comprehend. I think this is not as true as it once was; even when folks live in very small places, it is mostly a bedroom life with jobs and shopping elsewhere. But once upon a time it was possible to be born, live and die, all within the confines of a Belspring or Parrott and yet experience a fullness of life worthy of a book.

DEPUTY SHERIFF CAL MOORE warn't a man to mess with. That is my first and best description of him. For years Belspring and Parrott had no official law officers. The law, as people called the sheriff's department, had to drive the twenty-five miles from Pulaski to Belspring. Cal Moore solved that when he was appointed deputy sheriff and lived in Dry Branch, just down the river from Parrott. Now with Deputy Moore, the law was close at hand. He was as mean as the proverbial *rolling hoops snake*. Once, a guy, name forgotten, boarded at the Moores' place. The man awakened one morning with his throat slit—or rather he didn't awaken. The Moores' version of the facts steadfastly insisted he had cut his own throat and, maybe figuratively, the guy did cut his own throat by making a play for Cal's wife or daughter. Most folks suspected the wielder of the knife was none other than Cal himself, but only the foolish would say that in public. No one ever knew the real story and the official cause of death was suicide.

After his deputy sheriff days, Cal ran a small store in Elliston, a place in the road between Christiansburg and Roanoke. One morning, a man who Cal helped put in prison found him alone in the store and beat him within an inch of his life. The ex-prisoner bragged to the Montgomery County sheriff in Christiansburg: "I meant to larn him a lesson." Justice came hard in our little part of the world and I suppose Cal did larn a lesson.

WILLIAM LONG was a Belspring share-cropper with many children—twelve to be exact. He had so many children that the store porch gossip said the missus no longer took him into her bed and as a consequence, he developed an affection for his milk cow, but store porch gossip was just that, idle talk.

I best remember Old Man William as a Calhoun's Store-porch-preacher, which was his real love in life. He was an uneducated man, so his preaching was mostly shouting in the hard-breathing, country, Pentecostal style. His sermons were usually brought on when a bunch of boys ragged him enough. When the Spirit moved him, and his feet began to pound the boards on Calhoun's porch; it was a sight to see and hear. Made little sense, but it was right entertaining in the same manner as most revival preaching. Whether anyone listened or not, he preached up a storm and perhaps berated a sinner or two into the kingdom, though I never personally knew anyone who got saved by Old Man Long's shouting about getting right with God. Mr. Long was in his own way a good man and, even if not a preacher, he was a fascinating character worth remembering.

CHARLIE LONG OF HICKMAN CEMETERY ROAD was a blacksmith, house painter, carpenter, and jeweler—a man of many talents. One of Charlie's talents was to fix folks' broken, expensive watches. He had the watches running in no time at all. Everyone was pleased with his work until one of Charlie's customers took his watch to a Radford Jewelry store for repair. The jeweler's verdict: "Someone has replaced the jewels in your watch with painted wooden ones." Come to find out it was one of Charlie's best skills; his painted wooden jewels were first class, but they were wooden and didn't last.

His talent with watch jewels had folks up in arms, so Charlie was arrested and held in the Pulaski jail until trial time. Uncle Dick's living room was the court, so I stationed myself by an open window and took it all in. The verdict was guilty with prison time. Off went multi-talented Charlie to the Bland County Correctional Farm for a few months of growing vegetables and tending to cows. I suppose he came back to Belspring a changed man, maybe with even more talents than before, though he did give up watch repair.

ETHEL BRUCE was born Ethel Crawford in Belspring in 1893. She was a smart, hard-working, wise-in-the-ways-of-nature lady. When young, she married a Snyder and they had a brood of children. When he was killed in the Parrott Coal Mine, it was the days before Social Security and folks in Belspring/Parrott had no life insurance. She was left with small children and no money. The coal mine offered sympathy to the widow and young children, nothing more. So, Ethel made a living best she knew how. As a midwife she delivered at least fifty children, cutting the umbilical cord and giving the baby her first bath. At the other end of life, she cared for the dead. When folks passed away, families called for her and she washed the bodies and laid them out for viewing. She said of her work, "I wash them comin' and goin'." At other times, she washed and ironed neighbors' clothes, cleaned houses, and generally helped other people for a little money or a poke of potatoes. They in turn helped her and her children as best they could. Neighborliness was a fact of life in those bygone days. She was also known to take fire out of burns and warts off of hands, but she never charged for this medical care, or *white magic* as it was sometimes called. It was her gift—received and given.

When marriage was proposed by a Crigler fellow in Belspring, Ethel accepted, and they lived in the village for a short time. But the marriage didn't last, and they separated for reasons no one now knows. Clearly, she was smarter than he was, and other men took a fancy to her, including my dad, George Bruce. Shortly after Crigler, she went to Toledo, Ohio with Dad, her moon-faced Lothario, married him and became the only Mrs. Bruce— other than Mommie—we ever knew. I'm not sure if Ethel ever divorced Crigler before she and Dad married, but neither of them were big on ceremony. They were as married as they needed to be. It was the third and final marriage for both, an until-death-do-us-part union.

When Dad's health broke up in Ohio, they moved to Covington, Virginia to be near Ethel's sister. After Dad died, Ethel moved to Christiansburg, Virginia to be near her Snyder granddaughters. We saw her often in her apartment and then in the nursing home, where pushing toward the century mark she was chosen to be Mrs. Santa Claus in the Christiansburg Christmas Parade. She remained a life force, bright, intelligent, ever cheerful with the hint of white magic in her eyes.

When she died, she was buried beside Dad in the cemetery that looks down on Fairlawn and the Belspring/Parrott road. Home at last!

"Come home, come home, ye who are weary, come home."
"Softly and tenderly Jesus is calling – calling for you and for me.
Patiently Jesus is waiting and watching – watching for you and for me."

"Softly and Tenderly Jesus is Calling,"
Will L. Thompson, 1880

PART THREE

TRAVELING THE BELSPRING ROAD TO LATER LIFE

"God of our life, through all the circling years, we trust in thee… With each new day, when morning lifts the veil, we own Thy mercies, Lord, which never fail."

"God of Our Life, Through All the Circling Years,"
Hugh Thomson Kerr, 1916

CHAPTER 23

1934 – The End of My Childhood

"Sing them over to me again to me, wonderful words of life. Let me more of their beauty see, wonderful words of life. Let more of their beauty see, wonderful words of life."

"Wonderful Words of Life," Philip Bliss, 1874

GRADUATION FROM BELSPRING HIGH SCHOOL marked the end of my childhood. In 1934, no jobs were to be had in Belspring/Parrott, so I signed up for President Roosevelt's Civilian Conservation Corps (CCC). The government promised me $30 per month, of which I kept $5 and sent the rest home to Uncle Doley and Aunt Fanny.

In August of that year, I left Belspring behind and headed to Roanoke where I caught a train bound for Norfolk, Virginia. Once there, it was a boat ride to Fort Monroe Island. I lived with about forty other boys in an old Army barracks where we slept on cots, wore World War I uniforms, ate in the mess hall, and stood daily for dress and barracks inspection. We were 10,000 strong young men from here and there across the eastern United States: white boys from Appalachia, blacks from the coastal areas, and Yankees of one sort or another from where I could not imagine. We were a duke's mixture of races and sizes. To a boy away from home and on his own, it was bewildering. I was big-time homesick for Belspring, my own little spot in the world.

The good news was we were only to be in Fort Monroe for two or three days. The bad news was that someone came down with a contagious disease and all 10,000 of us were quarantined with nothing to do. To keep us busy, the camp commanders assigned us various tasks including weeding with hand sickles or moving 94-pound bags of cement, which was approximately what I weighed. We loaded the bags onto a truck and the trucks moved down to the next loading bay and we unloaded it. This schedule continued ten hours a day for two weeks. I was exhausted at the end of each day but was determined to carry my load no matter how small I was.

After about two weeks, twenty of us shipped out and headed for another camp in Scottsburg, Virginia near the North Carolina border. In total, there were 200 of us in that camp: twenty from Virginia and the others from New Jersey, Pennsylvania, or New York City. Several of the guys from New York City were called *spics*, a term I had never heard before. They were Spanish-speaking folks who were native to the Caribbean but came from New York City.

Our camp's assignment was to build Staunton River State Park including a swimming pool, bath house, picnic shelters, cabins, and outdoor fireplaces. That we did. For the good work we performed, we went on liberty to South Boston, Virginia. However, it was 1934 and Virginia was a very prejudiced state. The local folks raised so much *cain* over the presence of the spics that the CCC shipped all of them to another location. I never knew what happened to them, but I do remember that my biggest accomplishment of that night of liberty was that I looked so young, I got into the cinema on a child's ticket.

For Christmas I received a week's leave, so I rode the train to Radford. When I arrived at the Depot there was no one to meet me since I was the only one in our household who could drive. So, I walked the eight or nine miles to Belspring with great anticipation of seeing Uncle Doley and Aunt Fanny. It felt so good to be home for a few days.

I had no money when I left Belspring to go back to the camp; Doley bought me a ticket to South Boston. My train was late arriving in Lynchburg, so I missed the train to South Boston. There was only one train a day, so I waited twenty-four hours at the Lynchburg train station with no money and no food. Slept on the bench. By the time I got to South Boston, no one was waiting at the station for me there either, so I caught a ride on a bread truck that was headed to the camp. It had been almost two days since I had eaten so the mess hall smelled like heaven. Never had any food tasted better!

We were a good work group and soon finished our part of building the camp, so we went to another camp near Danville, Virginia to do soil conservation. A couple of things stand out in my memory of that place. One was a boxing match where I was paired with a small guy from New York. Weight wise, we were well matched, but he beat me forty ways from Sunday: I had black eyes, cuts on my lips, and a well-bloodied nose. Later I learned that the year before, he had been runner-up in his weight division in the Golden Gloves tournament in New York. As the saying goes, "I couldn't lay a hand on him." I am not sure how or why I agreed to fight him, but I was thoroughly humiliated, only to find out that lots of the other guys thought I was pretty gutsy to get in the ring with the Golden Glover.

My other chief memory was a July Fourth holiday—it must have been 1935 and we were given some leave from the camp. Along with two friends, one a Smith and one a Purdham, we went to a bootlegging joint in Danville for some whiskey. With moonshine in hand, we walked up a holler near a creek and sat on some rocks to enjoy our refreshment. After drinking a while, Smith and Purdham got into a fight over something and Purdham cut off Smith's necktie with a knife. I tried to break it up but the next thing I knew, I awakened, alone, with rain falling on my face. Smith and Purdham were nowhere to be seen. I had apparently been clocked on the head with a rock and thrown into the creek. Luckily, I landed on a sandbar or that might have been my last day on Earth. I still have the indentation in my skull from that rock.

My last CCC stop was Camp Catawba near Salem, Virginia. We worked up in the mountains building roads and fire trails and, if needed, fighting fires in the surrounding counties. Once in early spring, we blasted some rock off a curve and in the rocky rubble found a whole bunch of copperhead snakes. They were stiff and cold, almost like picking up a stick of wood—not that I tried it, mind you, but some of the boys did. I never did much like snakes and seeing them all coiled up together like that reminded me of the "brood of vipers" from the Bible and being condemned to Hell. Gave me the willies for sure.

While in Catawba, close to the end of my service I became extremely ill and spent a month in the Roanoke Memorial Hospital with a high fever. I was pretty much out of it for most of the time and ate and drank very little. Though I was already thin, I lost an additional twenty-five pounds and was skin and bones when I was dismissed.

Never did find out what ailed me, though folks said I cheated death again, just like in early childhood.

It was 1936 when I finished my time in the CCC. I was nineteen years old.

CHAPTER 24

Rose Ellen Smith:
The Love Bug Bites

By 1936, I was back from the CCC and living once more at Fanny and Doley's place while I worked on a paint crew with the Norfolk and Western Railway.

ON A LAZY, crystal clear autumn Sunday afternoon, I met my Rose Ellen: I was nineteen; she was thirteen, and it was love at first sight—a love that lasted until death did us part, sixty-four years later. That now long-ago day began with my old friend Charlie Linkous' invitation to ride with him to see his new girlfriend, Virginia Smith— all grown up at fifteen. On the way, he told me Virginia's younger sister was quite a looker, but I knew Charlie was full of blarney and baloney, so I laughed along with him.

We rattled our way down the Belspring Road in Charlie's antiquated, battered Ford dump truck, which he used to collect garbage in Belspring/Parrot to dump into the New River. We crossed the river on the circa 1900 wooden plank bridge, turned right on Main Street for a mile, took a left up the steep Bolling Street hill to the corner of Fifth and Bolling to the Smith place. It was a sprawling one-story white frame house surrounded by a picket fence that kept the chickens out of the road. There I met the love of my life.

Virginia was waiting in the front yard to meet us, not much fazed by the arrival of a dump truck. I barely noticed her however, because standing beside Virginia was her thirteen-year-old sister, Rose Ellen. I loved that beautiful young, freckle-faced girl from the moment I saw her. In that first meeting, Rosie and I talked a bit, though I could think of little to say to her; mostly I gawked at her loveliness.

Before Charlie and I piled back into his truck and headed home to Belspring, I told Rosie that when she got a little older I was coming back and marrying her. She giggled and then Charlie and I rattled away.

In the following years, most weeks I worked out of town from Monday through Saturday. These were the days before people were in constant touch by telephone, so Rosie and I didn't talk often. On Sundays, however, I had a standing invitation to the afternoon main meal. Fried chicken, mashed potatoes, green beans and biscuits were the order of the day, after which a hot apple pie was served. After lunch, we sat in the porch swing holding hands or walked through the orchard and down Fifth Street to Ingles Cemetery where we wandered among the headstones. By the time Rosie was sixteen, as soon as we could afford to begin housekeeping, we were bound to one another.

In July 1939, we married at the Methodist parsonage in the small community of New River. Rosie was sixteen and I was twenty-one. Rosie's sister, Virginia, and her new husband, Ed Bower, stood with us. For our honeymoon, we drove in our antiquated Plymouth Coupe the nine or ten miles to Christiansburg, holding hands the whole way. We stayed in a motel near what is now a custard stand on Route 8, but before we went to our room we ate country ham, green beans, and mashed potatoes for supper.

When it came time for our romantic encounter of the evening, Rosie was so scared she raised the window in our room and hopped out on the grass and ran off. I went after her and it took some mighty pleading on my part to get her to come back in the room. After a while, she settled down and we began what would be sixty-one years of a wonderful, adventurous marriage.

After our memorable wedding night, we were back on the Belspring Road for a month's stay with Aunt Fanny in my childhood home place. Rosie lived in the house with Fanny while I did shift work building the Radford Army Ammunition Plant, or the Arsenal, as it was locally referred to. Not too long after that, the apartment over Calhoun's Store became available, so I was able to rent it for us. As I recall, we paid $12.50 a month for two rooms, no bathroom or running water. Thinking about that now, it was a sparse lodging, not much really, but it was our place for just the two of us Three of my stout buddies, including Charlie Linkous, his brother Mutt, and my brother Clyde helped me carry whatever possessions we had up those narrow stairs including some furniture and a very heavy cast-iron stove. We barely made it up that one flight! Next door on the same floor was the big meeting room where the Belspring Chapter of the KKK held their meetings, complete with sheets and hoods.

During the day, while I was working at the Arsenal, Rosie stayed in Belspring with her friends Kathleen, Alta Mae, and Randolph. When possible, on the lawn across from the Presbyterian church, they laid on a blanket and smoked their Lucky Strikes, ate Nabs (Rosie's name for cheese crackers) and Hershey bars with almonds, and drank Cokes from the little glass bottles. They waved to every passerby, whether walking, riding or driving, and dreamed the wondrous dreams of youth.

In the ways of young lovers, those days were enchanted times for us. We drove our old Plymouth down to Parrott when the New River was in flood stage. Floating past us on the river were haystacks filled with chickens and pig litters stranded on top. Once an old barn shed went by with a cow or two inside! Those images have lingered as reminders of a simpler time. Daily, we laughed our way down the stairs of our apartment and went across the street to Tice's water pump where we filled our bottles and buckets and then waltzed back up the stairs to our own blue heaven.

After our marriage, our first supper guests were Rosie's parents, Lura and Estel Gray Smith. Rosie served ham, always her favorite, with mashed potatoes and a tiny bowl of macaroni and cheese. Later, her father confessed that he was afraid to take any of the macaroni and cheese because the serving bowl was so small it only allowed for one serving! We laughed over the years about her first attempt at entertaining and saved that bowl as a reminder. Rosie also baked a chocolate sheet cake for dessert; it was this cake that in later years our grandchildren called a choco-cake. What a wonderful life!

One of those nights on the second floor of Calhoun's Store, Rosie became pregnant with our first child, Robert (Bobby) Gray Bruce. When he was born in September 1941, our small apartment was no longer adequate, so we soon moved up the street to a little house owned by Ethel Snyder, who eventually became Ethel Bruce, Dad's wife. In that house, we had our own garden and a pigpen where we raised four meat hogs for butchering every year. Once, to our great delight during hog killing time, young Bobby Gray, then just a toddler, participated in the ritual by pretending to slit the throat of his ceramic piggy bank. It became a yearly practice for him every hog killing season. It is a picture happily etched in my memory.

"This is the day (and days) the Lord has made. Let us rejoice and be glad in it."

Psalms 118

CHAPTER 25

Fairlawn

*During the war years, the military contracts at the Radford Arsenal
continued to increase along the number of workers needed. The village of
Fairlawn was developed on an old apple orchard to house
the workers at a location convenient to the Arsenal.*

THE COMMUNITY OF FAIRLAWN became a
continuation of Belspring life for me and my Rose Ellen.
Due to my association with the Arsenal, it was our good
fortune in 1944 to purchase one of the small houses in
Fairlawn, seven miles down the Belspring Road.

Our house at 20 Orchard Road was a luxury: a
spacious front porch, a living room, a dining room, two
bedrooms with a shared indoor bathroom, a kitchen, a
back stoop, a yet-to-be-dug basement, plus sufficient yard
space for a garden. We were homeowners who had
attained the American dream with the monthly payment
of $24.25 for thirty years. The day we moved in I told
Rosie, "My next move is to the funeral home." It was
both promise and prophecy.

The Fairlawn of those years was an ideal place for a
young family. In 1947, our family of three grew with the
birth of our second son, George Stephen Bruce, known
by one and all as Steve. Bobby Gray and Steve were two
of the many children who lived in the neighborhood, so

no scarcity of friends for our boys. Within walking distance of our house was the Presbyterian church, which we joined and where I eventually served as a deacon and elder. Two grocery stores served as bookends for the village, with the Sutz-U Market and attached Fairlawn Sundry on one end and Looney's Store on the other. We even had an ESSO station, a hot dog stand and Simpson's Garage, whose owner, Mr. Simpson, had dreams of eventually converting it into a Tucker auto dealership. I once took my boys up to Simpson's Garage and we saw sketches of the Tucker 48. I, along with the other men of Fairlawn, shared the dream of owning one. Alas, Simpson's never acquired one of the fifty-one Tuckers that were produced. We were all left with only our fantasies.

My oldest son, Bobby Gray, attended first grade in the old, two-room schoolhouse, which was previously two chicken coops that were put together and turned into a school. It was replaced in time by a brand-spanking-new elementary school, with grades from first through seventh. The Riverlawn School was just a few blocks away from our house and all the neighborhood children walked to school together.

During these years I often worked out of town, so in my absence, Rosie and the boys spent many days in Radford with her momma, Lura. Rosie and Lura canned beans and tomatoes and often Rosie would cook supper for her folks. Bobby Gray and Steve spent time out in their yard chasing the chickens, collecting eggs, and exploring the farm.

Steve spent his early years without his daddy close at hand and was sometimes a handful for Rosie. When he learned to crawl, his worldview was mostly the floor. He would often lick his finger then run it under the refrigerator or furniture in the vicinity, to pick up whatever dirt was there. Then he promptly licked the contents from his finger. Rosie was horrified by this, so she took him to the doctor whose advice was typical of the time: "It won't hurt him so let him do it. He'll tire of it someday." And he did.

When I was home, I tried to be a good parent and teach Steve to be obedient. He didn't much appreciate this. I vividly remember the time he dumped all his Tinkertoys in the floor to play. When it came time for supper, I told him to pick them up and put them in the box. His reply was simple: "No, I not!" The standoff escalated. I asked again, and again he refused, so I spanked him. He still refused to pick up a single toy. I was reduced to taking his hand, opening his fingers and closing them over each toy, then opening them to drop the toys in the box. This was repeated for every Tinkertoys on the floor. Steve was a good and loving boy, but he was one stubborn little cuss. Rosie told me he was just like me, but I don't believe I was ever that tenacious.

As they grew older, both boys were good athletes. Steve was a tough and tenacious linebacker; Bobby Gray was an excellent passer and quarterback on the only unbeaten and untied football team Dublin High School ever had. Rosie and I were proud as punch of our boys.

Life was good! Rosie had girlfriends on every street; the boys ran free, coming home only to eat and sleep. We played baseball in the front yard until Steve planted a tree in the middle of it, then the game moved to the back yard. Hide and go seek, kick the can, or catching fireflies were the rituals of each day and evening for our family and friends. I gardened to my heart's content, growing corn, half-runner beans, tomatoes and cabbages, as well as beautiful roses—for my Rose Ellen.

One of my favorite hymns in those days summarized the way I feel about Fairlawn and remains one I still sing to myself:

"Count your blessings, name them one by one.
Count your blessings, see what God has done.
Count your blessings, name them one by one.
Count your many blessings, see what God has done!"
"Count Your Blessings," Johnson Oatman, 1897

CHAPTER 26

Precious Memories,
How They Linger

The weaving together of remembrances that have spanned over eighty-plus years culminated with several generations overlooking a hill in Belspring – in gratitude for the past and goodly hope for the future.

ON A COLD FEBRUARY DAY IN 2007, I stood on the porch of the long-deserted Buckland's Store, site of the old Belspring Post Office, and looked down the snowy hill on Kirkwood land. About 1927, I sleighed down that hill while the joy and goodness of life flooded through me as strongly as I've ever known it.

On that long-ago day of childhood, I knew I had made it through the darkness of Mommie's death and absence. I knew beyond a shadow of doubt that life was good, almost impossibly good, and that the future opened for me in ways I could only faintly imagine.

As I remember that day when I was ten years old, I can still feel the cold wind on my face as I raced down the hill. Oh, the exhilaration as I turned sharply left and missed going into the cold water of the branch! I can over the years yet hear the shouts of "Way to go, Bobby!" from those at the top of the hill. Maybe, just maybe, I can be fortunate enough in these last years of my life to keep some small part of the wonder of those moments in my eyes and ears.

How good life has been to me. How fortunate I was to live in Belspring and Fairlawn and be married to Rose Ellen and have two sons and six grandchildren and three great-grands with hopefully more on the way. I have loved my life and my people. I am grateful to God and eagerly look forward to glad reunions on that morning we meet again across the generations and begin a long stretch of living in Beulah land.

"I'm living on the mountain underneath a cloudless sky, oh yes, I'm drinking from the fountain that never shall run dry. And I'm feasting on the manna from a bountiful supply, for I am dwelling in Beulah land."

Charles Austin Miles, 1911

Robert Wilson Bruce, 1917–2009

EPILOGUE

GENEALOGY

Family Tree

Abbreviated

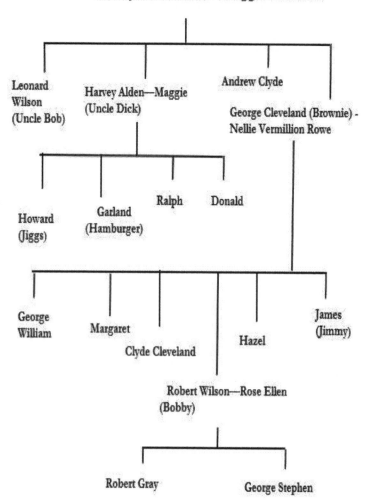

Harvey Howe Bruce—Maggie E. Burton

Leonard Wilson (Uncle Bob)

Harvey Alden—Maggie (Uncle Dick)

Andrew Clyde

George Cleveland (Brownie) - Nellie Vermillion Rowe

Howard (Jiggs)

Garland (Hamburger)

Ralph

Donald

George William

Margaret

Clyde Cleveland

Hazel

James (Jimmy)

Robert Wilson—Rose Ellen (Bobby)

Robert Gray

George Stephen

The Bruce Clan History

*This is an oral genealogy, quite unscientific and unproven, of my particular
Bruce clan. It is an outline of how they came to Belspring in 1880. I
know only bits and pieces of my ancestry and it is almost entirely
patriarchal, which I regret. I leave it to future generations to correct and
put flesh on these bones.*

TO PARAPHRASE James Weldon Johnson's great
poem/hymn: *"My Bruce clan has come over a way that with
tears [and hopes] has been watered."* Like most immigrants to
this country, it was a long, hopeful, rough journey that my
Bruce ancestors made...and the road finally brought
them and me to Belspring, Virginia.

Some of our more recent family history is well known.
It is a fact that Grandfather Harvey Howe Bruce of
Walkers Creek—in present day Bland County, Virginia—
married Maggie Burton of Highland Road, Pulaski
County, in 1880. He was twenty, she twenty-six. That
year, they set up housekeeping in Belspring on Depot
Street, in a house gifted to them by her parents, the
Burtons. In that Depot Street house, she gave birth to
their four sons: Leonard Wilson (Uncle Bob), Harvey
Alden (Uncle Dick), Andrew Clyde (Uncle Clyde),
George Cleveland (Brownie, my dad). Granddaddy
Harvey died in 1889, and Maggie raised the four boys on
her own. She died in 1917, so I never had the privilege of
knowing either of my Bruce grandparents. But there was

a mystique about the land and places of Belspring that gave me a sense of my heritage.

When my six-times great grandfather George Bruce (perhaps George L. or George William) left Scotland, he traveled many weeks across the sea, and came ashore in Maryland sometime in 1710. He could not imagine what joy and heartache awaited his extended family. Though I do not know the real story of this George Bruce, there are hints he may have come from a prominent, early settlement family from which he was disowned or disinherited because of some mystery or disgrace that followed him. Unfounded family rumor is that George, as an old man, may have moved to the southwestern Virginia mountains and was buried in an area of Slide Mountain in present-day Bland County, in the Bruce Family Cemetery owned by his grandson, Joshua Bruce, a Methodist preacher.

According to old man Andrew Marion Bruce of Newport News, Virginia, who grew up near the Slide Mountain and is a part of my family tree somewhere down the line, I first heard that George's son, my five-times great grandfather, William L. Bruce, lived in Surrey County, North Carolina. There he was a property owner and fought on the colonist's side in the Revolutionary War. He died in 1813 or 1814 and is supposedly buried in the same Slide Mountain Cemetery as his father, George (if in fact George is buried there). So far as I know, the cemetery is long abandoned and forgotten.

William L.'s oldest son, Vincent, born about 1773, married Elizabeth Hearn and they are my four-times great grandparents. In family tales, I also learned that in 1816–1817, at age forty-four Vincent Bruce—with wife Elizabeth and some of their offspring—left the family property near Walkers Creek, Virginia and headed north to the southern Ohio areas of Gallia and Lawrence Counties. They may have left because the year of 1816 was without a summer (also called the poverty year), when there was snow and frost remaining in late July in the high mountains. Even in good years, crops were sparse in the Virginia mountains, but with a cold summer, it meant no crops at all and the very real possibility of hunger and starvation in Walkers Creek. Current knowledge informs us that this fluke of weather and nature was caused by an enormous volcanic eruption in Indonesia in 1815.

So, with hunger and starvation on their heels, it was onward to the Ohio River in the hopes that farming and life would be easier in an altitude not so steep and rocky. Gallia County, Ohio became home and the cemetery in Greenfield Township in Lawrence County became their final resting place; Vincent died in 1839 and Elizabeth in 1846. I have never seen their graves. When I learned that my family was in both southern Ohio and the mountains of Virginia, it was not hard to imagine that cousins may have fired at one another in the Civil War. What I know for certain is that Vincent and Elizabeth's grandson, William Amos Bruce, fought for the Confederates in the Civil War and was wounded in the skirmish at White Sulphur Springs in present-day West Virginia. It is this William Amos Bruce and his wife Barbary Ellen who were the parents of my grandfather Harvey Howe Bruce, who settled in Belspring in 1880.

It is through this oral history and family tales that I know my ancestors were participants in the great migrations and battles of our nation that gives a broader perspective to my life in Belspring than I knew when I was young. As the biblical writer expressed it about deep matters of the spirit:

"Since we are surrounded by so great a cloud of witnesses, let us run with perseverance the race that is set before us."

Hebrews 12:1

When I came to Belspring to live in 1926, little could I have dreamed that all this history would beckon and follow me, but *this too is my story, this too my song* and I hope future generations know it.

FAMILY PICTURES

*Mommie and
Bobby –1917*

*Family portrait, circa 1918.
Brother Clyde, Father George Cleveland,
sister Margaret, Mommie, Robert Wilson*

Nellie's Gravestone

"Gone But Not Forgotten"

Aunt Fanny and Uncle Doley Caldwell's home in Belspring where Bobby lived through high school.

Bobby Bruce
School picture
Circa 1928

Aunt Fanny Caldwell
1930's

Bobby with the car he drove Uncle Doley to the mine in every morning

Harvey A. Bruce
(Uncle Dick)
Circa 1948

Bobby Bruce
School picture
Circa 1932

George Cleveland Bruce
Circa 1948

Engineer Leonard Wilson Bruce (Uncle Bob)
in Bluefield, West Virginia.
January 15, 1952 by Train #15, Engine 611.

Young Leonard Wilson
with ax
Circa 1900

Clyde - 1932

Belspring Norfolk & Western
Train Depot

Hog-killing time at Malley Whitlock's

*Old Man
John Harkrader*

*Jack Carden with Bobby's nephew Wallace Bruce
and his son, Todd,
after his first haircut.*

Etta Long, center, behind Etta, Josephine Giles Bruce (Clyde's wife), to the right, Gerline Smith (Rose Ellen's sister), and Lura Smith, (Rosie's mother) far right.

Remaining steeple from Belspring Methodist Church

Bob Caldwell, Center
Circa 1945

The five adult siblings together in 1946.
Bobby, Hazel, Jimmy, Margaret, and Clyde Bruce

Ethyl Bruce
Circa 1975

Bobby and
Rosie's
Wedding Day
July 29, 1939

Rose Ellen Smith at age 13

Rosie at Claytor Lake
Circa 1940

The Belspring Methodist Church Reunion
Circa 1945

Fairlawn house with Rose Ellen, Bobby Gray,
Aunt Margaret, and Fluffy

Bobby with his dad, George Cleveland on the porch of the Fairlawn house

*Son Robert Gray Bruce, Robert Wilson Bruce,
great grandson Jacob Wilson Bruce,
grandson Robert Gray Bruce, Jr., 2003*

THE BELSPRING ROAD

ACKNOWLEDGMENTS

Chief editor, cover designer, encourager, loving wife – Laurie
Cartographer, editor – son, Robert G. Bruce, Jr.
Photos – daughter, Shannon Elizabeth Bruce Stosser
and son-in-law, David Fisk

All of our children, including daughter, Casey and son, Adam,
have been helpful and supportive throughout this process and have
patiently endured reading various versions and re-writes of the book.

Over the years, various people have read my journals and encouraged me to publish these stories. Mike Murray, Arnold Sykes, and the Mo-Ranch "No Help At All Gang"—to whom the stories were first read—have heard many versions, and to them I am most grateful.

Kristen Hamilton performed my final editing, proofing, formatting and gave me direction through the publishing process.

CreateSpace folks made the publishing process as simple as could be possible.

All of these and many others who are unnamed are contributors to this book reaching publication and I thank them all.

Made in the USA
Middletown, DE
01 March 2019